Contemporary

American

Architects

Volume IV

Philip Jodidio

Contemporary **American** Architects

Volume IV

TASCHEN

KÖLN LISBOA LONDON NEW YORK PARIS TOKYO

Page 2 | Seite 2
Richard Meier, Getty Center, Los Angeles,
California, 1984–97. A detail of the cleft travertine
cladding.

Richard Meier, Getty Center, Los Angeles,
Kalifornien, 1984–97. Detail der
Fassadenverkleidung aus ungeschliffenem Travertin.

Richard Meier, Getty Center, Los Angeles,
Californie, 1984–97. Détail du revêtement extérieur
en travertin rugueux.
© J. Paul Getty Trust/Photo: Scott Frances/Esto

© 1998 Benedikt Taschen Verlag GmbH
Hohenzollernring 53, D-50672 Köln

Edited by Christine Fellhauer, Cologne
Design: Sylvie Chesnay, Paris
Cover Design: Catinka Keul, Cologne
French translation: Jacques Bosser, Paris
German translation: Annette Wiethüchter, Berlin

Printed in Italy
ISBN 3-8228-7426-4

Contents | Inhalt | Sommaire

An Architecture of Circumstances
American Architects at the End of the 1990s

Eine Architektur der Gegebenheiten
Amerikanische Architekten Ende der 90er Jahre

Une architecture de circonstance
Architectes américains à la fin des années 90

The time of eclecticism in contemporary architecture is not yet finished. In fact, an almost bewildering variety of currents and styles seems to run in often diametrically opposed directions. As in art, there is no dominant approach to designing buildings. Rather given circumstances, or specific personal styles developed by architects, govern form more than any school of thought. The projects retained for this book vary in scope and budget from Richard Meier's Getty Center in Los Angeles to houses for the poor built by Sambo Mockbee and the Rural Studio in Alabama. The issues touched on by these buildings may be directly related to ecological concerns, as is the case of the Demonstration Home and Workplace in Austin, Texas, conceived by the Center for Maximum Potential Building Systems (CMPBS), or they may spring from a desire to reconcile the past and present, as does François de Menil in his Byzantine Chapel in Houston, Texas. Local circumstances and an architectural *parti pris* give rise to new projects by Eric Owen Moss and Steven Ehrlich in the urban sprawl of Los Angeles, while magnificent natural settings and substantial budgets have permitted I.M. Pei in the spectacular Miho Museum near Shigaraki, Japan, or Michael Rotondi and Clark Stevens in the Teiger House in New Jersey to break new aesthetic ground. The stylistic mark of great architects like Pei, Meier or Gehry clearly transcends the commonplace, but voices are also rising to claim that the responsibility of architecture to the environment should be allowed to go so far as to dictate forms for the future. Economic pressures in other cases impose such drastic restrictions that architects must entirely renew their palette of materials, forms and construction methods. Necessity in these circumstances is indeed the "mother of invention."

Earth, Wind and Fire
Throughout the years of Postmodernism, Richard Meier maintained his adherence to a pure geometry related to the work of such architects as Le Corbusier. More than almost any other living American architect, he is identified with a signature style, a white purity, and a rigor all his own. His reputation was based

Noch ist die eklektische Stilperiode der Gegenwartsarchitektur nicht vorbei. Tatsächlich sieht es so aus, als würden sich verwirrend viele unterschiedliche Strömungen und Stile in oft völlig entgegengesetzte Richtungen entwickeln. Wie in der Kunst hat sich auch in der Architektur keine einzelne Entwurfskonzeption durchgesetzt. Stärker als jede Theorie bestimmen örtliche Gegebenheiten oder der persönliche Stil des jeweiligen Architekten die Form. Die in diesem Buch vorgestellten Bauten sind in Bezug auf Größe und Kosten ganz unterschiedlich – von Richard Meiers Getty Center in Los Angeles bis hin zu den von Sambo Mockbee und dem Rural Studio in Alabama errichteten Wohnungen für die Armen. Die Bauaufgaben beinhalten Themenstellungen wie Ökologie – etwa im Fall des Musterhauses mit Arbeitsplatz in Austin, Texas, des Architekturbüros namens Center for Maximum Potential Building Systems (CMPBS) – oder entspringen dem Wunsch, Geschichte und Gegenwart zu verbinden, wie es François de Menil mit seinem Byzantine Chapel Museum in Houston tat. Örtliche Gegebenheiten und festgefügte Auffassungen haben Eric Owen Moss und Steven Ehrlich dazu geführt, im zersiedelten Stadtrandgebiet von Los Angeles neue Projekte zu realisieren. Phantastische natürliche Standorte und großzügige Budgets ermöglichten es demgegenüber I.M. Pei mit seinem spektakulären Miho Museum bei Shigaraki in Japan oder Michael Rotondi und Clark Stevens mit ihrem Teiger House in New Jersey, ästhetisch neue Wege zu gehen. In stilistischer Hinsicht übertreffen die Bauten großer Architekten wie Pei, Meier oder Gehry bei weitem das Mittelmaß. Es sind aber auch schon Stimmen laut geworden, denen zufolge es zur Verantwortung der Architektur gegenüber der Umwelt gehört, neue Bauformen für die Zukunft zu diktieren. In anderen Fällen führen wirtschaftliche Zwänge zu so drastischen Restriktionen, daß Architekten völlig neue Baustoffe, Formen und Baumethoden einsetzen müssen.

Erde, Wind und Feuer
In den Jahren der Postmoderne blieb Richard Meier bei seiner reinen Geometrie ganz im Sinne solcher Architekten wie

*I.M. Pei, Miho Museum, Shigaraki, Shiga, Japan,
1992–97. A typical detail shows the juncture between
the stonework and the space frame structure of the
skylights.*

*I.M. Pei, Miho Museum, Shigaraki, Shiga, Japan,
1992–97. Ein typisches Detail zeigt die Nahtstelle
zwischen Natursteinmauerwerk und dem Raumfach-
werkrahmen der Oberlichter.*

*I.M. Pei, Musée Miho, Shigaraki, Shiga, Japon,
1992–97. Détail caractéristique de la jonction entre
l'appareillage de pierre et la structure tridimensionnelle
des verrières.*

Pour l'architecture contemporaine, la période de l'éclectisme
n'est toujours pas achevée. En fait, une étonnante variété de
courants et de styles perdure, dans des directions diamétrale-
ment opposées. Comme dans le domaine artistique, aucune
tendance ne domine les autres. Ce sont davantage les circonstances particulières ou les styles personnels spécifiques des
architectes qui déterminent les formes qu'une quelconque école
de pensée. Les réalisations sélectionnées pour cet ouvrage
couvrent donc une grande diversité de projets et de budgets,
allant du Getty Center de Richard Meier à Los Angeles, aux
logements pour exclus de Sambo Mockbee et du Rural Studio
en Alabama. Les enjeux qu'illustrent ces projets peuvent d'une
part être directement liés à des préoccupations écologiques,
comme dans le cas de la «maison-lieu-de-travail de démonstration» à Austin, Texas, érigée par un groupe d'architectes nommé
Center for Maximum Potential Building Systems (CMPBS).
Ils peuvent d'autre part également provenir d'un désir de
réconcilier le présent et le passé, comme dans le cas de François
de Menil et son chapelle-musée des fresques byzantines à
Houston, Texas. Les circonstances locales et un parti-pris
architectural affirmé expliquent la genèse des nouveaux projets
d'Eric Owen Moss et de Steven Ehrlich dans la conurbation de
Los Angeles, tandis que des sites naturels magnifiques et des
budgets substantiels donnent l'occasion à I. M. Pei dans son
spectaculaire Musée Miho, près de Shigaraki au Japon, ou à
Michael Rotondi et Clark Stevens dans la Teiger House au
New Jersey d'explorer des esthétiques nouvelles. La marque
stylistique des grands architectes comme I. M. Pei, Richard
Meier ou Frank O. Gehry transcende clairement les règles
communes, mais des voix s'élèvent également pour proclamer
que la responsabilité de l'architecture par rapport à l'environnement doit aller jusqu'à dicter les formes de l'avenir. Dans
d'autres cas, les pressions économiques imposent des contraintes si drastiques que les architectes se voient obligés de
renouveler entièrement leur palette de matériaux, de formes
et de méthodes de construction. Dans ces cironstances,
la nécessité est bien en effet la «mère de l'invention».

Richard Meier, Rachofsky House, Dallas, Texas, 1991–96. Multiple screens assure privacy, yet the residential function of this structure is not readily apparent.

Richard Meier, Rachofsky House, Dallas, Texas, 1991–96. Zahlreiche Blendwände schützen den privaten Bereich. Daß dieses Gebäude ein Wohnhaus ist, erschließt sich allerdings nicht auf den ersten Blick.

Richard Meier, Rachofsky House, Dallas, Texas, 1991–96. De multiples écrans assurent l'intimité, sans que la fonction d'habitation ne soit trop évidente pour autant.

in part on private residences, like the spectacular Douglas House (Harbor Springs, Michigan, 1971–73), perched above the shores of Lake Michigan. And yet since the Grotta House (Harding Township, New Jersey, 1984–89), Richard Meier had not completed another residential commission. It was a visit to the High Museum in Atlanta in the 1980s that encouraged Howard Rachofsky, a Texas businessman, to ask the architect to design a house for him. But Meier's first proposal was not to be built. As Rachofsky says, "The building died of its own weight." According to him, it was too big for the site, "way too expensive," and couldn't house his collection of art. A divorce in 1989 prompted the Texan to go back to Meier with a new site and a different list of priorities, which in due time produced an acceptable design. "The Rachofsky House," says Richard Meier, "represents an ideal, an investigation into all the possibilities of house as a building type, without many of the usual compromises. In this sense, I suppose, the Rachofsky House is a case study, inducing us to look at and think about what our own notions of house and home encompass." Howard Rachofsky, it seems, was willing to pay the price, in every sense of the word, to create a masterpiece. "Being a perfectionist," he says, "I was not willing to quit until the details were right... I had wonderful role models in Dallas: the Rose House by Antoine Predock is a wonderful building; the Price House by Steven Holl is a really interesting, controversial piece of architecture. I wanted to be part of that lineage and make this a community destination."[1] Like most of Meier's successful buildings, the Rachofsky House is suffused with light. Filled with art, it is akin to a small museum. It is above all the kind of architectural jewel that Richard Meier has always excelled in designing, finely crafted in the white harmonies he prefers.

Two very ambitious private houses built on opposite sides of the United States by the founding partners of Morphosis, who have since gone their separate ways, speak to a very different set of priorities, even if they share with Richard Meier the goal of creating exceptional works of architecture in a residential mode. The Blades Residence (Santa Barbara, California, 1992–96) by

Le Corbusier. Mehr als jeder andere lebende amerikanische Architekt wird er bzw. sein Werk mit einer ganz spezifischen »Architekturhandschrift« identifiziert, einer reinweißen Strenge, die nur ihm eigen ist. Sein Ruf gründete sich zunächst vor allem auf Einfamilienhäuser, etwa dem eindrucksvollen Douglas House (Harbor Springs, Michigan, 1971–73), das auf einer Anhöhe am Ufer des Michigan-Sees liegt. Nach dem Grotta House (Harding Township, New Jersey, 1984–89) hat Richard Meier jedoch kein weiteres Privatwohnhaus verwirklicht. Howard Rachofsky, Geschäftsmann aus Texas, beauftragte Meier nach einem Besuch im High Museum in Atlanta in den 8oer Jahren, ihm ein Haus zu entwerfen, doch dessen erster Entwurf sollte nicht gebaut werden. Rachofsky sagte dazu: »Das Haus ging an seinem Übergewicht zugrunde«. Er fand es zu groß für das Grundstück, »viel zu teuer«, und es bot keinen Platz für seine Kunstsammlung. Nach seiner Scheidung 1989 wandte sich der Texaner erneut an Meier mit einem neuen Grundstück und einer anderen Prioritätenliste, wobei der Entwurf dieses Mal schließlich angenommen wurde. »Das Rachofsky House«, so Meier, »stellt ein Ideal dar, Ergebnis der Untersuchung sämtlicher Möglichkeiten eines Wohnhauses als Bautyp, und ohne die vielen üblichen Kompromisse. In diesem Sinne ist das Rachofsky House wohl eine Fallstudie, die uns veranlaßt, unsere Vorstellungen von Wohnung und Zuhause zu überdenken.« Howard Rachofsky war offenbar bereit, den Preis im wahrsten Sinne des Wortes für ein Meisterwerk zu bezahlen. Er sagte: »Ich bin ein Perfektionist und wollte nicht locker lassen, bis alle Details vollkommen waren... In Dallas fand ich hervorragende Vorgänger: Das Rose House von Antoine Predock ist ein herrliches Gebäude, und Steven Holls Price House ist ein wirklich interessantes, kontroverses Stück Architektur. Mein Haus sollte in dieser Erbfolge stehen und diese Art des Bauens zur öffentlichen Zielsetzung werden lassen.«[1] Wie die meisten gelungenen Meier-Bauten ist auch das Rachofsky House lichtdurchflutet. Mit Kunstgegenständen angefüllt, gleicht es einem kleinen Museum. Vor allem ist es genau die Art Architektur-Juwel, mit der sich Richard Meier immer hervorgetan hat,

La terre, le vent, le feu

Tout au long des années de règne du postmodernisme, Richard Meier est resté fidèle à une géométrie épurée, proche de l'œuvre d'architectes comme Le Corbusier. Plus que n'importe quel autre praticien vivant, il s'est identifié à un style – sa signature – tout de pureté et de rigueur. Sa réputation repose en partie sur des résidences privées comme la spectaculaire Douglas House (Harbor Springs, Michigan, 1971–73), perchée au-dessus du lac Michigan. Et cependant, depuis sa Grotta House (Harding Township, New Jersey, 1984–89), Meier n'avait pas exécuté la moindre commande de résidence privée. C'est une visite au High Museum d'Atlanta dans les années 80 qui a encouragé l'homme d'affaires texan Howard Rachofsky à demander à l'architecte de lui dessiner une maison. Mais la première proposition de Meier ne devait pas avoir de suite. Comme le dit Rachofsky: «Le bâtiment s'est étouffé sous son propre poids». Selon lui, il était trop grand pour le site, «beaucoup trop cher», et ne pouvait accueillir sa collection d'œuvres d'art. Son divorce en 1989, le poussa à retourner voir Meier avec un nouveau terrain et une liste de priorités différentes qui, avec le temps, engendrèrent un projet accepté. «Rachofsky House», explique Richard Meier, «représente un idéal, une investigation de toutes les possibilités qu'offre une maison en tant que type de construction, sans la plupart des compromis habituels. Dans ce sens, cette réalisation est un cas d'étude, qui nous encourage à regarder et à réfléchir à ce que recouvrent nos notions de maison et de foyer.» Howard Rachofsky, semble-t-il, était prêt à payer le prix, dans tous les sens du mot, pour créer un chef-d'œuvre. «Étant un perfectionniste», dit-il, «je ne voulais pas abandonner tant que tous les détails n'étaient pas parfaits... J'avais sous les yeux de superbes références à Dallas: la Rose House d'Antoine Predock qui est une merveilleuse réalisation, ou la Price House de Steven Holl, une création architecturale controversée et passionnante. Je voulais me rattacher à tout ceci et faire de ce projet une œuvre marquante au bénéfice de la collectivité.»[1] Comme la plupart des réalisations réussies de Meier, la Rachofsky House est imprégnée de lumière. Remplie également

Thom Mayne and Morphosis, and the Teiger House (Somerset County, New Jersey, 1990–95) by Michael Rotondi and his new partner Clark Stevens of RoTo are both intensely related to the sites they are built on. Whereas the Rachofsky House seems to sit lightly on the land, a beacon of geometric perfection, the Blades and Teiger houses dig into the earth and seem to emerge from it, opposing angular complexity to Meier's minimalist purity.

When Richard Blades, a California artist, and his wife returned to their home in Santa Barbara after a brief trip in June 1990, they discovered that their ranch-style house had been completely destroyed by fire. Having visited the Crawford House (Morphosis, Montecito, California, 1987–92), they called on Morphosis principal Thom Mayne to design a new residence, which would take into account the site, but also avoid the dangers of the kind of explosive fire which had destroyed their previous home. Thom Mayne described this 750 square meter house as follows: "A large exterior room has been created within which the house is situated. This room embraces an augmented natural landscape conveying a sense of sanctuary... Through the fusion of the exterior and interior worlds, the individual gradually becomes oriented... learns to keep balance... The building arrangement, while alluding to the specific characteristics of this site, ultimately demonstrates its tentativeness to fixity by making overt reference to our temporary status as occupants." In the completed house, spaces are intended to "bleed" into each other with no precisely marked point of transition. Thom Mayne has declared that the "modernist penchant for unification and simplification must be broken." Indeed, the work of his group has emphasized the importance of societal changes, such as the growing role of electronic communications, and the "breakdown of a conventional notion of community." This analysis would appear to be clearly at odds with that of a Richard Meier.

It is, however, in harmony with the latest work of Morphosis co-founder Michael Rotondi in New Jersey. If the Blades Residence and the Teiger House share many characteristics, it is no accident. As David Teiger says of Michael Rotondi, "I visited

sorgfältig errichtet in den von ihm bevorzugten »weißen Harmonien«.

Zwei aufwendig gestaltete Einfamilienhäuser im Osten und im Westen der USA – entworfen und gebaut von den Gründungspartnern des Büros Morphosis, Thom Mayne und Michael Rotondi, die seither getrennte Wege gehen – erfüllen eine ganz andere Prioritätenliste, selbst wenn sie Richard Meiers Zielsetzung folgen, außergewöhnliche Architektur im Wohnhausbau zu schaffen. Die Entwürfe zur Blades Residence (Santa Barbara, Kalifornien, 1992–96) von Thom Mayne und Morphosis, und zum Teiger House (Somerset County, New Jersey, 1990–95) von RoTo, d.h. Michael Rotondi und seinem neuen Partner Clark Stevens, sind beide eng auf ihren Standort und Baugrund bezogen. Das Rachofsky House scheint den Boden nur leicht zu berühren, der Inbegriff geometrischer Perfektion, die Häuser von Blades und Teiger sind dagegen in die Erde eingegraben, die eckige Komplexität der aus dem Boden aufsteigenden Teile steht im Kontrast zu Meiers minimalistischer Reinheit.

Als der kalifornische Künstler Richard Blades und dessen Frau nach einer Kurzreise im Juni 1990 wieder in ihr Haus nach Santa Barbara zurückkehrten, fanden sie ihr Haus vollkommen niedergebrannt vor. Da sie das von Morphosis 1987–92 in Montecito, Kalifornien, gebaute Crawford House kannten, beauftragten sie Thom Mayne, den Chef von Morphosis, mit dem Bau eines dem Grundstück angepaßten neuen Wohnhauses mit eingebautem Brandschutz gegen die Art verheerenden Feuers, das ihr erstes Haus zerstört hatte. Thom Mayne beschreibt seinen Entwurf zum Neubau mit 750 m² Wohnfläche folgendermaßen: »Ein großer Außenraum wurde um das Haus herum geschaffen. Er umfaßt eine angereicherte natürliche Landschaft, die ein Gefühl von Heiligtum vermittelt... Infolge der Fusion von Außen- und Innenwelt orientiert sich der Mensch allmählich, ... lernt, sein Gleichgewicht zu halten. Während es auf die Charakteristika des Baugeländes anspielt, vermittelt das Haus in Gliederung und Form letztlich sein Zögern, sich festzulegen, indem es deutliche Anspielungen auf unseren temporären

d'œuvres d'art, c'est presque un petit musée, et, par dessus tout, le type de joyau architectural dans lequel Richard Meier a toujours excellé, avec une exécution raffinée dans les harmonies blanches qu'il préfère.

Deux très ambitieuses résidences privées, édifiées sur les deux côtes opposées des États-Unis par les associés fondateurs de Morphosis – qui suivent aujourd'hui chacun leur propre route –, expriment des priorités bien différentes, même si elles partagent avec Meier l'objectif de créer des œuvres architecturales résidentielles d'exception. La Blades Residence (Santa Barbara, Californie, 1992–96) par Thom Mayne de Morphosis, et Teiger House (comté de Somerset, New Jersey, 1990–95) par Michael Rotondi et son nouvel associé, Clark Stevens de RoTₒ, entretiennent toutes deux des relations intenses avec le site sur lequel elles s'élèvent. Si Rachofsky House semble délicatement posée sur son terrain, image même de la perfection géométrique, les Blades et Tiger Houses s'enterrent et semblent du coup émerger du sol, opposant leur complexité angulaire à la pureté minimaliste de Meier.

Lorsque Richard Blades, un artiste californien, et sa femme revinrent chez eux à Santa Barbara après un court voyage en juin 1990, ils découvrirent que leur maison de style ranch avait été entièrement détruite par un incendie. Après avoir visité Crawford House (Morphosis, Montecito, Californie, 1987–92), ils firent appel au principal associé de Morphosis, Thom Mayne, pour concevoir un projet qui prenne en compte le site bien sûr, mais aussi les risques d'incendie, cause de la destruction de leur précédente demeure. Thom Mayne décrit cette maison de 750 m² de la façon suivante: «Une vaste pièce extérieure a été créée, à l'intérieur de laquelle se trouve la maison. Elle inclut un paysage naturel enrichi qui donne un sentiment de sanctuaire... Par la fusion des mondes extérieur et intérieur, l'individu subit peu à peu une influence... apprend à garder son équilibre... Les aménagements de la construction, tout en se référant aux caractéristiques spécifiques du site, démontrent sa tendance à l'immuabilité en faisant ouvertement référence à notre statut temporaire d'occupants.» Dans la maison achevée, les espaces

Morphosis, Blades Residence, Santa Barbara, California, 1992–96. A house intended to "embrace the natural landscape."

Morphosis, Blades Residence, Santa Barbara, Kalifornien, 1992–96. Ein Haus, das die »natürliche Landschaft umarmen soll«.

Morphosis, Blades Residence, Santa Barbara, Californie, 1992–96. Une maison qui veut «englober le paysage naturel».

the Crawford House, which was then under construction in Montecito, and there was something primal about it – it really moved me spiritually. I responded to that house so much that I hired him." From this common point of origin – the Crawford House, designed by Morphosis when Mayne and Rotondi were still working together – the two architects have created very different works. The Teiger House is extraordinarily complex. Rotondi explains, "We once looked for ways to cram experience into structure that were created graphically or abstractly. Here, for the first time, we started with experiential things – light, sun, connection to the ground – and not with some abstract order. Theory didn't drive this house. It came after the fact."[2] Though it has connections to the work of such varied architects as Carlo Scarpa and Frank O. Gehry, the Teiger House in a way looks back to the legacy of Frank Lloyd Wright. It is, as its owner says, intended to be "of the land and not on the land."[3] This intention is made clear both in the siting of the house, at the top of a knoll is at a juncture between forest and field, offering a view reaching almost 50 kilometers into the green countryside, and in the presence of such elements as a living room hearth incorporating an outcropping of existing stone. Aesthetically, the contrast with Meier's Grotta House, located very close by, could not be stronger, although both homes are fundamentally designed to live with their magnificent natural settings. Like Meier's client Howard Rachofsky, David Teiger took a very real interest in what can only be described as the creation of a work of art to live in, selecting RoTo over twenty other firms consulted. Like Rachofsky, Teiger divorced two years into the project, changing many of the specifications outlined in a twenty-five page document.

The Good, the Modest and the New
Though related to their sites, the Rachofsky, Blades and Teiger houses are separated from the main stream of architecture by their very circumstances. Built with high budgets and a concern for architectural quality, they are by definition set outside of the circumstances of the "real" world. At the opposite end of the economic spectrum, efforts are being made to adapt con-

Status als Bewohner macht.« Im fertigen Haus sollen Räume ohne markante Übergänge »ineinanderübergehen«. Thom Mayne hat erklärt, daß »die moderne Neigung zu Einheitlichkeit und Vereinfachung gebrochen werden muß«. Die Arbeit dieser Architektengemeinschaft hat tatsächlich die Notwendigkeit zu gesellschaftlichen Veränderungen betont, etwa infolge der zunehmend wichtigen Rolle der elektronischen Kommunikation und des »Zusammenbruchs traditioneller Vorstellungen von Gemeinschaft«. Diese Analyse scheint Richard Meiers Diagnose deutlich zu widersprechen.

Sie stimmt jedoch überein mit dem letzten Bau von Michael Rotondi in New Jersey. Daß die Häuser für Blades und Teiger vieles gemeinsam haben, ist kein Zufall. So sagte David Teiger über Michael Rotondi: »Ich sah mir das Crawford House an, als es in Montecito gebaut wurde. Es hatte so etwas Ursprüngliches und berührte mich tief. Das Haus sprach mich auf einer geistig-spirituellen Ebene so stark an, daß ich ihn [Rotondi] engagierte.« Aus dieser gemeinsamen Grundlage – dem Crawford House von Morphosis, als Mayne und Rotondi noch zusammenarbeiteten – haben die beiden Architekten ihre ganz unterschiedlichen Bauten entwickelt. Das Teiger House ist außerordentlich komplex. Rotondi erklärt dazu: »Früher versuchten wir, Erfahrung in Konstruktionen hineinzustopfen, die graphisch oder abstrakt konzipiert worden waren. Hier gingen wir zum ersten Mal von Erlebniswerten aus – Licht, Sonne, Bodenhaftung – und nicht von einer abstrakten Ordnung. Dieses Haus ist nicht von der Theorie her gestaltet, die kam erst nach den Fakten.«[2] Obwohl es Bezüge zu den Werken so unterschiedlicher Architekten wie Carlo Scarpa und Frank O. Gehry aufweist, blickt das Teiger House in gewisser Weise auf das Erbe Frank Lloyd Wrights zurück. Wie sein Besitzer sagt, soll es »vom Lande und nicht auf dem Lande«[3] sein. Diese Absicht ist ablesbar an der Plazierung des Hauses auf einem Hügel an der Grenze zwischen Wald und Feld, mit einer fast 50 km weit reichenden Aussicht in die grüne Landschaft und an Elementen wie einem Wohnzimmerkamin, der einen vorhandenen natürlichen Felsvorsprung umfaßt. In ästhetischer Hinsicht könnte

RoTo, Teiger House, Somerset County, New Jersey,
1990–95. A very complex design.

RoTo, Teiger House, Somerset County, New Jersey,
1990–95. Ein höchst vielgestaltiger Entwurf.

RoTo, Teiger House, Somerset County, New Jersey,
1990–95. Une conception très complexe.

«coulent» les uns dans les autres, sans point de transition
nettement marqué. Thom Mayne a déclaré que «le penchant
moderniste à l'unification et à la simplification doit être brisé».
Et il est certain que le travail de son groupe s'attache à prendre
en compte les changements de la société, tels le rôle grandissant
de la communication électronique et «la rupture de la notion
conventionnelle de communauté». Cette analyse semble par-
faitement opposée à celle d'un Richard Meier.

Elle est, en revanche, en harmonie avec la dernière réalisation
du co-fondateur de Morphosis, Michael Rotondi, dans le
New Jersey. Ce n'est pas un hasard si Blades Residence et Tiger
House partagent de nombreuses caractéristiques. Comme le
précise David Teiger en parlant de Rotondi: «J'ai visité Crawford
House qui était alors en construction à Montecito, et il y avait
là quelque chose d'originel qui m'a spirituellement touché.
J'ai tellement adhéré à ce projet que j'ai eu envie de faire appel à
lui.» Partant d'un point d'origine commun, puisque Crawford
House avait été conçue par Morphosis lorsque Mayne et Rotondi
travaillaient encore ensemble, les deux architectes ont créé deux
œuvres très différentes. Teiger House est extraordinairement
complexe. Rotondi s'explique ainsi: «Jadis, nous cherchions à
faire entrer toutes nos expériences dans une seule structure
créée graphiquement ou abstraitement. Ici, pour la première
fois, nous avons commencé par expérimenter des réalités – la
lumière, le soleil, la connexion avec le sol – et non pas seulement un ordre abstrait. Ce n'est pas la théorie qui anime cette
maison. Elle n'est venue qu'après le fait.»[2] Bien qu'elle ne soit
pas sans rapport avec les travaux d'architectes aussi divers que
Carlo Scarpa et Frank O. Gehry, Teiger House, d'une certaine
façon, regarde vers Frank Lloyd Wright. Comme le précise son
propriétaire, elle est «du sol et non sur le sol»[3]. Cette intention
s'affirme à la fois dans l'implantation, au sommet d'une butte
à la jonction de la forêt et des champs qui offre une vue sur la
campagne jusqu'à près de 50 km à la ronde, et dans la présence
d'éléments comme l'âtre du living-room qui incorpore un
morceau de rocher préexistant. Esthétiquement, le contraste
avec la Grotta House de Meier, toute proche, ne pourrait être

Center for Maximum Potential Building Systems, Advanced Green Builder Demonstration, Austin, Texas, 1994–97. Esthetics which emerge from the ecological program developed by the designers.

Center for Maximum Potential Building Systems, Advanced Green Builder Demonstration (Musterhaus mit häuslichem Arbeitsplatz), Austin, Texas, 1994–97. Die Ästhetik der Architektur als Ergebnis des ökologischen Programms der Architekten.

Center for Maximum Potential Building Systems, Advanced Green Builder Demonstration, Austin, Texas, 1994–97. Une esthétique particulière, conséquence du programme écologique développé par les architectes.

temporary architecture to situations that are closer to the living conditions of ordinary people. These efforts naturally have to do with ecological concerns, but also the fact that very few people can actually afford to call on talented architects.

Significantly, one very interesting challenge to assumptions about architectural form and function is being made by a group called the Center for Maximum Potential Building Systems (CMPBS) in Austin, Texas. Its two principals are indeed more interested in the possibilities of an ecologically oriented type of construction than they are in theory or aesthetics. Pliny Fisk III was trained as an architect at the University of Pennsylvania, but he went on to take a degree in landscape architecture, with an emphasis on "ecological land planning." His partner, Gail Vittori, is specialized in energy research and waste management, hardly a typical profile in the architectural world. Their Demonstration Home and Workplace or Advanced Green Builder Demonstration "is a 170 square meter publicly accessible environmental building exhibit located on the outskirts of Austin, Texas. The project grew out of our organization's collaboration with the City of Austin to create the Austin Green Builder Program, which was the only U.S. program recognized at the 1992 Rio Earth Summit." Here, every phase of the project, from construction materials to disassembly system, is conceived with the greatest possible concern for the environment. Rather than Portland cement, which "contributes nearly 9% of total CO_2 output... the building uses a non-Portland cement substitute, based on 97% recycled materials and aggregates (fly ash and bottom ash), with impressive structural properties." The post and beam structure of the house is made from "98% recycled steel based on crushed automobiles." The operation of the building is conceived in similar terms. According to the designers, "Because Central Texas is subject to droughts, we sized water collection sufficient for a family (or office) of four people using ultra conservation practices, and since wastewater treatment is a major energy user by our city we treat our wastewater on site using wetlands and other plants as a kind of wastewater landscape to help cool our structure while retaining precious nutrients within the soil." Together with

der Kontrast zu Meiers Grotta House ganz in der Nähe nicht krasser sein, obwohl beide Häuser auf das Wohnen in dieser wunderschönen Landschaft hin angelegt worden sind. Wie Meiers Bauherr Howard Rachofsky war auch David Teiger sehr daran interessiert, etwas zu bekommen, was man nur ein Kunstwerk zum Bewohnen nennen kann, und gab RoTo den Vorzug vor 20 anderen bereits konsultierten Architekturbüros. Wie Rachofsky ließ sich auch Teiger zwei Jahre nach Inangriffnahme des Projekts scheiden und änderte dann viele Punkte der 25-seitigen Anforderungsliste.

Gut, bescheiden und neu

Obwohl sie sich in ihre Umgebung einfügen, unterscheiden sich die Häuser von Rachofsky, Blades und Teiger durch ihre Baukonditionen von den meisten anderen Wohnhausbauten. Die Bauherren verfügten über großzügige Budgets und wünschten eine hohe architektonische Qualität, ihre Häuser übersteigen schon allein deswegen den Rahmen der normalen Verhältnisse. Am anderen Ende des ökonomischen Spektrums gibt es Bestrebungen, die Gegenwartsarchitektur entsprechend den Lebensverhältnissen der Normalbürger zu realisieren. Diese Bemühungen betreffen natürlich u.a. ökologische Lösungen, berücksichtigen aber auch die Tatsache, daß nur sehr wenige Leute es sich leisten können, hochtalentierte Architekten zu engagieren.

Das Architekturbüro Center for Maximum Potential Building Systems (CMPBS) mit Sitz in Austin, Texas, hat bisherige Annahmen zu architektonischer Form und Funktion auf ganz interessante Weise in Frage gestellt. Die beiden Chefs interessieren sich mehr für die Möglichkeiten einer ökologischen Bauweise als für Architekturtheorien und ästhetische Aspekte. Pliny Fisk III. studierte Architektur an der University of Pennsylvania und absolvierte dann ein Studium in Landschaftsarchitektur mit Schwerpunkt »ökologische Baulandplanung«. Seine Partnerin Gail Vittori ist auf Energieforschung und Abfallentsorgung und -verwertung spezialisiert – nicht gerade das typische Berufsbild des Architekten. Ihr Musterhaus mit

plus marqué, même si les deux maisons sont conçues en fonction de leur magnifique cadre naturel et pour en bénéficier. Comme le client de Meier, Howard Rachofsky, David Teiger s'est réellement intéressé à ce que l'on peut décrire comme une «œuvre d'art à vivre», sélectionnant RoTo parmi plus de 20 agences. Ainsi que Rachofsky, Teiger a divorcé alors que le projet était déjà en route depuis deux ans, ce qui a amené à modifier les nombreuses spécifications précisées dans un document de 25 pages.

Le bon, le modeste, le nouveau

Bien qu'étroitement intégrées à leur site, les résidences Rachofsky, Blades et Teiger figurent à l'écart du courant général actuel de l'architecture du fait des circonstances mêmes de leur création. Bénéficiant de budgets élevés et d'un grand souci de qualité, elles ont par leur nature et leur origine rien à voir avec le bâti «réel». À l'opposé du spectre économique, des efforts sont en cours pour adapter l'architecture contemporaine à des situations plus proches des conditions de la vie ordinaire. Ces tentatives intègrent naturellement des préoccupations écologiques, mais aussi la simple réalité qui veut que peu de gens peuvent se permettre de faire appel à des architectes de talent.

Il est significatif que l'un des plus intéressants défis lancé aux présupposés formels et fonctionnels de l'architecture ait été lancé par un groupe appelé Center for Maximum Potential Building Systems (CMPBS), originaire d'Austin au Texas. Ses deux responsables sont, en fait, plus intéressés par les possibilités d'une construction de sensibilité écologique que par la théorie ou l'esthétique. Pliny Fisk III a reçu une formation d'architecte à l'Université de Pennsylvanie, mais est également titulaire d'un diplôme d'architecture du paysage, orienté sur «la planification écologique du sol». Son associée, Gail Vittori, est spécialisée dans les recherches sur l'énergie et la gestion des déchets, profil assez rare dans le monde de l'architecture. Leur maison et lieu de travail de démonstration est un bâtiment d'exposition de 170 m², ouvert au public dans la banlieue

a systematic application of such methods to energy and resource usage, the Demonstration Home and Workplace is conceived to be highly flexible. "The bathroom (referred to as the Carousel Bathroom) can rotate in order to enable a series of privacy configurations in a very small space. The living room combination work room can be transformed from desks to presentation space to a dinner table suited for twelve people to a dancing space including an area for the music band. The kitchen (Meals on Wheels) can be plugged in at the east wing or the central breezeway but can also be brought right onto the dance floor as a buffet kitchen and again plugged into that location." The implication of this radical concept is that appearance evolves from a series of functional and design choices related to a very responsible and contemporary conception of life styles and collective needs.

The approach to the problems of contemporary architecture chosen by Sambo Mockbee and Dennis Ruth, two professors of architecture at Auburn University, is quite different. Sensing the need of his students to escape from the cloistered, theoretical environment that is typical of current architectural education in the United States, he created the Rural Studio. This project is intended to allow twelve students at a time from Auburn to go to Greensboro, Alabama, where they design and build houses for the poor living in Hale County. With support from the Alabama Power Foundation and other private sources, the Rural Studio's aim has been to provide decent homes for people who have spent their lives in metal sheds. "We are doing this in the exact place where James Agee and Walker Evans lived in the 1930s when they documented the miserable truth of the sharecropper's lives in 'Let Us Now Praise Famous Men'. It's not much different now. The needs are so great."[4] Amongst the structures completed by the Rural Studio, the 80 square meter Bryant House, built out of such unexpected materials as hay and clear acrylic, cost only $16,500 paid for through grants and donations. Another project, the Harris House, uses recycled pine and corrugated metal arranged, as Mockbee says, "like a big screened porch" with a "butterfly" roof encouraging natural air circulation. Finally, the group made inventive use of 1,000 used automobile tires

Arbeitsplatz (Advanced Green Builder Demonstration) »ist ein öffentlich zugängliches ökologisches Ausstellungsobjekt mit 170 m² Fläche am Stadtrand von Austin, Texas. Das Projekt entwickelte sich aus der Zusammenarbeit unserer Organisation mit der Stadt Austin zur Schaffung des Austin Green Builder Program [Programm für Grünes Bauen], das als einziges US-Programm an der Umwelt-Gipfelkonferenz 1992 in Rio de Janeiro anerkannt wurde«. Bei der Planung und dem Bau dieses Hauses wurden in jeder Phase – von der Baustoffauswahl bis zur Demontage – mit größter Sorgfalt ökologische Aspekte berücksichtigt. Anstatt Portland-Zement zu verwenden, der »fast 9% des gesamten CO_2-Ausstoßes produziert, ... wurde für das Gebäude ein Zementersatz aus 97% wiederaufbereiteten Materialien und Zuschlägen (z.B. Flugasche und Hochofenschlacke) mit eindrucksvollen konstruktiven Eigenschaften verwendet«. Die Ständerbaukonstruktion des Hauses besteht aus »98% wiederaufbereitetem Stahl aus Autoschrott«. Der Betrieb des Gebäudes folgt ähnlichen Vorgaben. Die Architekten erklären: »Da es in Zentral-Texas Dürreperioden gibt, berechneten wir Wassersammelbecken für eine vierköpfige Familie (oder Büromannschaft), die äußerst sparsam mit Wasser umgeht; da die Abwasserreinigungsanlage unserer Stadt ein Haupt-Energieverbraucher ist, behandeln wir unsere Abwässer vor Ort, indem wir Feuchtbiotope und Pflanzen als eine Art Rieselfeld nutzen. Diese tragen zur Kühlung des Hauses bei und halten auch die kostbaren Nährstoffe im Boden.« Im Verbund mit einer systematischen Anwendung von Sparmethoden in Bezug auf Energie und andere Rohstoffe ist das Musterhaus mit Arbeitsplatz äußerst flexibel konzipiert. »Das Badezimmer (Karussellbad genannt) läßt sich drehen, um eine Reihe von abgeschirmten Bereichen auf kleinstem Raum herzustellen. Der Wohnraum – zugleich Arbeitszimmer – kann umfunktioniert und ummöbliert werden: vom Büro mit Schreibtischen zum Raum für Präsentation, zum Eßzimmer für zwölf Personen oder zur Tanzfläche mit Platz für die Band. Die Küche »Essen auf Rädern« kann im Ostflügel angeschlossen werden oder im zentralen offenen Verbindungsgang, sie kann aber auch auf die

d'Austin. Le projet né d'une collaboration entre l'agence et la municipalité a donné naissance au «Austin Green Builder Programme», le seul programme américain retenu lors du Sommet de la Terre de Rio de Janeiro (1992). Ici, chaque phase du processus de construction, des matériaux au démontage éventuel, est conçue dans le plus grand respect possible de l'environnement. Plutôt que du ciment de Portland, qui contribue à près de 9% aux émissions de CO_2, le bâtiment utilise un substitut de ciment aux possibilités structurelles remarquables, composé à 97% de matériaux et d'agrégats recyclés (suies et cendres). La structure à poutres et piliers de la maison est «à 98% en acier recyclé récupéré sur des automobiles.»

Le fonctionnement du bâtiment est conçu en termes similaires. Selon ses concepteurs «parce que le centre du Texas est sujet à la sécheresse, nous avons déterminé de façon rigoureuse la collecte d'eau suffisante pour une famille (ou un bureau) de quatre personnes, et puisque le traitement des eaux usées est l'une des grandes causes de consommation d'énergie de notre ville, nous traitons nos propres eaux sur site par épandage ou plantations, dans une sorte de paysage actif, conçu d'ailleurs pour contribuer à conserver la fraîcheur de la maison tout en maintenant les éléments nutritifs précieux dans le sol.» Parallèlement à une application systématique de méthodes de conservation de l'énergie et d'utilisation des ressources naturelles, cette maison se veut hautement polyvalente. «La salle de bains (appelée «Carousel Bathroom») pivote sur elle-même pour permettre une série de configurations intimes dans un très petit espace. Le living-room ou espace de travail voit ses plans de travail transformés en table de salle-à-manger pour environ douze personnes ou en espace de danse comprenant même un emplacement pour un orchestre. La cuisine («Meals on Wheels») peut se brancher dans l'aile est ou dans le passage central, mais également sur la piste de danse pour former un buffet.» Ce concept radical implique que l'apparence soit déterminée par une série de choix fonctionnels et conceptuels dans l'esprit d'une conception responsable et contemporaine des styles de vie et des besoins collectifs.

Sambo Mockbee and the Rural Studio, Bryant House (top), Yancey Chapel (bottom), Mason's Bend, Alabama, 1995–97. Built essentially by students, both structures use readily available materials, sometimes obtained through scavenging.

Sambo Mockbee mit Rural Studio, Bryant House (oben) und Yancey Chapel (unten) in Mason's Bend, Alabama, 1995–97. Für beide Konstruktionen – im wesentlichen von Studenten entworfen und gebaut – wurden Materialien verwendet, die leicht und billig erhältlich waren, zum Teil vom Schrottplatz.

Sambo Mockbee et le Rural Studio, Bryant House (en haut), Yancey Chapel (en bas), Mason's Bend, Alabama, 1995–97. Construites pour l'essentiel par des étudiants, ces deux structures font appel à des matériaux disponibles localement, voire même de récupération.

Thompson and Rose, Atlantic Center for the Arts, New Smyrna Beach, Florida, 1994–97. This view of the roofs emphasizes the presence of the surrounding vegetation.

Thompson and Rose, Atlantic Center for the Arts, New Smyrna Beach, Florida, 1994–97. Ein Blick über die Dächer zeigt die vegetationsreiche Landschaft.

Thompson and Rose, Atlantic Center for the Arts, New Smyrna Beach, Floride, 1994–97. Cette vue des toits met en valeur la forte présence de la végétation environnante.

donated by a local resident who had been ordered to clear his land of them. Three of the students had the idea of building an open air chapel with a corrugated tin roof and walls made from stucco-covered tires. The Yancey Chapel, located in Mason's Bend, Alabama, has much of the light, airy feeling also seen in the Bryant and Harris houses. Just as it gives students some ideas of the technical and financial difficulties involved in architecture, the Rural Studio also addresses one of the most obvious needs in the United States – that of inventing new ways to house the rural poor in decent, inexpensive homes. Indeed, few well-known architects in America have ever felt that they had any responsibility towards the country's poor. This makes Sambo Mockbee's Rural Studio all the more important.

One of the hallmarks of the work of younger architects both in the United States and throughout the developed world is their acceptance of project conditions that might well have frightened away older practitioners. More frequent, of course, is the problem of extremely low budgets. Charles Rose and Maryann Thompson, a husband and wife team in their mid 30s, have worked since 1992 on the Atlantic Center for the Arts, a "working retreat for artists" located near the city of Daytona (Florida) in an area of dense jungle-like vegetation. They have conceived a series of distinct structures, each one adapted to the art form it is intended for, connected by a boardwalk, like a "work of conceptual art," or again, like Katsura (imperial residence, Kyoto, Japan, 17th century) in its apparently random order. Calling for wood frame structures, set on concrete piers, the program extends to a total of about 1,000 square meters of space, or 1,550 square meters including the boardwalks, with a budget of $3 million. Light, and well integrated into its vegetal environment, the Atlantic Center for the Arts shows a pragmatic, creative side to American architecture that cannot be said to be typical of the older generation.

Chapels of Darkness and Light

We are constantly told that ours is an age without spirituality, one in which religion no longer has a well-defined place. Curiously,

Tanzfläche geschoben und dort eingestöpselt werden, wo sie dann zur Küchenbar wird.« Die Folgerung aus diesem höchst ungewöhnlichen Entwurfskonzept ist, daß sich das Erscheinungsbild aus einer Reihe funktionaler und gestalterischer Entscheidungen ergibt, welche wiederum Bezug nehmen auf eine sehr verantwortliche, zeitgemäße Auffassung von Lebensstil und gemeinschaftlichen Bedürfnissen.

Sambo Mockbee und Dennis Ruth, Professoren für Architektur an der Auburn University, gehen ganz anders an die Aufgabenstellung der Gegenwartsarchitektur heran. Mockbee spürte, daß seine Studenten aus der abgeschiedenen, rein theoretisch orientierten Universitätsatmosphäre herauskommen mußten, die für die Architektenausbildung in den USA heute so typisch ist, und gründete daher das Rural Studio. Dieses Projekt soll es jeweils zwölf Studenten aus Auburn ermöglichen, für eine bestimmte Zeit in Greensboro, Alabama, am Entwurf und Bau von Häusern für die Armen des Hale County praktisch mitzuarbeiten. Mit Unterstützung der Alabama Power Foundation und anderer privater Sponsoren arbeitet das Rural Studio an der Erstellung angemessener Unterkünfte für Menschen, die bis dato in Blechschuppen gelebt haben. »Wir tun dies an genau dem Ort, wo James Agee und Walker Evans in den 30er Jahren ihre Reportage ›Let Us Now Praise Famous Men‹ über die ›sharecroppers‹ [Amerikanische Landpächter, die ihre Pacht mit der Ernte bezahlen] und deren elende Lebensumstände erstellten. Heute ist es nicht viel anders. Die Not ist sehr groß.«4 Das von Rural Studio gebaute Bryant House (80 m² Wohnfläche) aus so ungewöhnlichen Materialien wie Stroh und transparentem Acryl kostete nur 16 500 $, die durch Spenden und Darlehen aufgebracht wurden. Beim Harris House, das – so Mockbee – »wie eine große Veranda mit Windschutzscheiben und Schmetterlingsdach« aussieht, verwendete das Rural Studio Pinienholzteile aus Abbruchhäusern und Wellblech. Schließlich verwertete die Gruppe 1000 alte Autoreifen, ein »Geschenk« eines Ortsbewohners, der sein Land gemäß behördlicher Auflage von ihnen befreien mußte. Drei der Studenten hatten die Idee, eine kleine Kapelle aus verputzten Autoreifen mit Well-

L'approche des problèmes de l'architecture contemporaine choisie par Sambo Mockbee et Dennis Ruth, deux enseignants en architecture d'Auburn University, est assez différente. Sentant le besoin des étudiants d'échapper à un environnement cloisonné et théorique qui est le propre de l'enseignement actuel de l'architecture aux États-Unis, ils ont créé le «Rural Studio». Ce projet permet chaque année à douze étudiants d'Auburn de séjourner à Greensboro, Alabama, pour dessiner et construire des maisons pour les pauvres du comté de Hale. Avec le soutien de l'Alabama Power Foundation et d'autres organismes privés, le but du Rural Studio est d'offrir des foyers corrects à des gens qui ont passé leur vie sous des abris de tôle. «Nous faisons ceci à l'endroit exact où James Agee et Walker Evans vécurent dans les années 30, lors de leurs recherches sur la vie misérable des journaliers agricoles qui parurent sous le titre de ‹Let Us Now Praise Famous Men›. Ce n'est pas très différent aujourd'hui. Les besoins sont tout aussi grands.»4 Parmi les constructions achevées par Rural Studio, Bryant House (80 m²), construite en matériaux aussi inattendus que du foin et du plastique acrylique transparent, n'a coûté que 16 500 $ financés par des bourses et des donations. Un autre projet, Harris House, fait appel au pin et au métal rouillé recyclé pour former, comme le précise Mockbee, «une sorte de grande véranda à écran» avec un toit en ailes de papillon qui facilite la circulation naturelle de l'air. Le groupe a également fait un usage inventif de 1000 pneus de voiture offerts par un habitant qui avait été sommé de les ôter de son terrain. Trois des étudiants ont eu l'idée de construire une chapelle en plein air à toit en tôle ondulée et murs en pneus recouverts de stuc. On retrouve dans la Yancey Chapel de Mason's Bend, en Alabama, le sentiment de lumière et d'espace bien aéré des Bryant et Harris Houses. Tout en donnant aux étudiants des aperçus plus concrets sur les difficultés techniques et financières qu'implique toute construction, Rural Studio s'attaque à l'un des besoins actuels les plus évidents des États-Unis: inventer de nouveaux types de logements décents pour les familles pauvres des zones rurales. En fait, peu d'architectes américains connus se sont jamais senti la moindre responsabi-

however, some of the most inspiring works of contemporary architecture are linked precisely to the tradition of worship, albeit often in an ecumenical or non-denominational way. With Tadao Ando in Japan or Mario Botta in Europe, small chapels have offered a form of expression whose power and presence is undeniable.

Steven Holl, who was born in 1947 in Bremerton, Washington, is currently completing the Museum of Contemporary Art in Helsinki. The subtlety of his approach both in intellectual and aesthetic terms sets him apart from many other contemporary American architects. He is a "thinking man's" architect, who has proven his ability to adapt his work to extremely rigorous budgetary situations. The Jesuit Chapel he recently completed for Seattle University is an example of this approach. "We were originally one of several architects invited to Seattle University to be considered for this project," says Steven Holl. "There were five finalists and we each had to give a public lecture at Seattle University. At the beginning of the lecture I admitted not being Catholic, but that I believed firmly in the power of architecture to form a religious space. I also admitted that I had never built a chapel before."[5] Using a vocabulary of relatively simple forms, and of light, Steven Holl designed this chapel along the lines inspired by the structure of the Jesuits' own faith. "The metaphor of light," says Holl, "is shaped in different volumes emerging from the roof, whose irregularities aim at different qualities of light. The concept, a gathering of different lights, can be seen in the concept sketch of bottles of light emerging from a stone box (see page 91). Just as no single method is prescribed in the Jesuits' spiritual exercises, here a unity of differences is gathered into one. Each of the light volumes corresponds to a part of the program of Catholic worship. The south-facing light corresponds to the procession, a fundamental part of the mass. The city-facing north light corresponds to the Chapel of the Blessed Sacrament and to the mission of outreach to the community."[6]

Steven Holl brought original solutions to budgetary constraints in this chapel. As he explains, "There was not a budget for stained glass. We made a series of color fields with back-painted baffles

blechdach zu bauen. Die Yancey Chapel in Mason's Bend, Alabama, hat viel von dem leichten, luftigen Flair, das auch die Häuser der Familien Bryant und Harris auszeichnet. Das Rural Studio vermittelt den Studenten nicht nur eine Vorstellung von den technischen und finanziellen Aufgaben des Architekten, sondern sucht nach neuen Möglichkeiten zur Lösung einer der dringendsten öffentlichen Aufgaben der USA, nämlich angemessenen, billigen Wohnraum für die arme ländliche Bevölkerung zu schaffen. Tatsächlich haben nur wenige bekannte amerikanische Architekten sich jemals in irgendeiner Weise für die Armen ihres Landes verantwortlich gefühlt. Daher ist die Arbeit von Sambo Mockbees Rural Studio um so wichtiger.

Die jüngeren Architekten in den USA und in allen hochentwickelten Ländern zeichnen sich dadurch aus, daß sie Projektbedingungen akzeptieren, die ältere Kollegen vielleicht abgeschreckt hätten. Am häufigsten ist natürlich das Problem extrem niedriger Budgets. Charles Rose und Maryann Thompson, ein Architekten-Ehepaar, beide Mitte dreißig, arbeiten seit 1992 am Projekt des Atlantic Center for the Arts, einem »Arbeits-Refugium für Künstler« in der Nähe der Stadt Daytona (Florida) mitten in einem Gebiet dichter, dschungelartiger Vegetation. Sie haben eine Reihe klar unterschiedlicher Einzelgebäude entworfen, deren jedes sich der Kunstform anpaßt, der es gewidmet ist. Alle sind durch einen Plankenweg miteinander verbunden, wie »ein konzeptuelles Kunstwerk« oder wie der Katsura-Palast (Kyoto, Japan, 1. Hälfte 17. Jh.) in seiner scheinbar zufälligen Ordnung. Die Ausschreibung forderte Holzrahmenbauten auf Betonpfeilern, ungefähr 1000 m² Nutzfläche bzw. 1550 m² Gesamtfläche inklusive Plankenweg. Dafür stand ein Budget von 3 Millionen $ zur Verfügung. Leicht und gut in seine grüne Umgebung eingefügt, zeigt das Atlantic Center for the Arts eine pragmatische, kreative Seite der amerikanischen Architektur, die für die ältere Generation von Architekten nicht typisch ist.

Kapellen der Dunkelheit und des Lichts
Ständig hören wir, daß wir uns in einer Epoche ohne Spiritualität befinden, in der die Religion keinen festen Platz mehr hat.

lité envers les catégories sociales défavorisées de ce pays, ce qui rend l'expérience du Rural Studio et de Sambo Mockbee d'autant plus importante.

L'un des points communs des travaux des jeunes architectes, aux États-Unis comme dans tout pays développé, est qu'ils acceptent des conditions de projets qui pourraient effrayer des praticiens plus mûrs. Le problème des budgets extrêmement serrés est l'un des plus fréquents. Charles Rose et Maryann Thompson, un couple d'architectes d'une trentaine d'années, travaillent depuis 1992 sur le projet de l'Atlantic Center for the Arts, «un lieu de retraite pour artistes», situé près de la ville de Daytona, Floride, dans une zone où la végétation fait penser à une jungle. Ils ont conçu une série de structures distinctes, chacune adaptée à une forme d'expression artistique particulière, réunies par un cheminement de planches, comme «une œuvre d'art conceptuelle», ou comme à Katsura (résidence impériale, Kyoto, Japon, XVIIᵉ siècle) dans un ordre apparemment aléatoire. Réalisé à partir d'ossatures de bois montées sur des socles de béton, le programme compte environ 1 000 m² d'espace, ou 1 550 m² si l'on inclut les passages. Le budget s'est élevé à 3 millions de $. Léger et bien intégré à son environnement végétal, l'Atlantic Center for the Arts montre l'un des aspects pragmatiques et créatifs de l'architecture américaine qui ne fait certainement pas partie des préoccupations des générations précédentes.

Chapelles d'ombre et de lumière

Il est souvent écrit que notre époque aurait perdu toute spiritualité et que la religion n'y trouverait plus sa place... Curieusement, quelques-unes des œuvres les plus inspirées de l'architecture contemporaine se relient cependant précisément à des traditions religieuses, bien que souvent dans une optique œcuménique ou sans étiquette précise. Les petites chapelles de Tadao Ando, au Japon, ou de Mario Botta, en Europe, nous proposent une expression dont la puissance et la présence sont indéniables.

Steven Holl, né en 1947 à Bremerton, Washington, achève actuellement le Musée d'art contemporain d'Helsinki. La subti-

Steven Holl, Chapel of St. Ignatius, Seattle University, Seattle, Washington, 1994–97. Two drawings by the architect emphasize the use of light.

Steven Holl, St. Ignatius-Kapelle, Seattle University, Seattle, Washington, 1994–97. Zwei Zeichnungen des Architekten zeigen seinen Umgang mit Licht.

Steven Holl, Chapelle Saint-Ignace, Université de Seattle, Seattle, Washington, 1994–97. Deux dessins de l'architecte qui illustrent son travail sur la lumière.

François de Menil, Byzantine Fresco Chapel Museum, Houston, Texas, 1991–96. An exterior view shows the austere concrete façades of the structure built to house fragments of frescoes originally executed in Cyprus.

François de Menil, Kapellen-Museum für byzantinische Fresken, Houston, Texas, 1991–96. Eine Außenansicht zeigt die schmucklosen Betonfassaden des Gebäudes, das speziell für die aus Zypern stammenden Fresken-Fragmente gebaut wurde.

François de Menil, chapelle-musée des fresques byzantines, Houston, Texas, 1991–96. Vue de l'extérieur des austères façades de béton de ce bâtiment, construit pour abriter des fragments de fresques d'origine chypriote.

and inset a single piece of stained glass of a complementary color in the midst of each." A similar technique was used by Holl in his offices for D.E. Shaw and Company (New York, NY, 1991). In the place of stone walls, which would have been too costly, tilt-up concrete was used, "just like Schindler's King's Road House."

The Byzantine Chapel erected by François de Menil in Houston has a very different point of origin than Holl's Jesuit Chapel in Washington. His mother, Dominique de Menil, is one of the best known patrons of the arts both in the United States and in Europe. It was largely through her efforts that the famous Rothko Chapel (Philip Johnson), together with the Menil Collection Museum and more recent Cy Twombly Gallery (both of these latter structures by Renzo Piano), came to be concentrated in the Montrose area of Houston, Texas. It was in 1983 that Dominique de Menil became interested in the fate of two 13th century Byzantine frescoes which had been removed from a chapel in a disputed area of Cyprus. After having the paintings restored, the Menil Foundation came to an agreement with the Greek Orthodox Bishopric of Cyprus, whereby the works could be placed on extended loan to Houston, at least until the situation on Cyprus allowed their return. In a move demonstrating the sensitivity of the foundation to the fate of art objects, the chapel that was built to house them and the land it is set on were given to the Greek Orthodox Church. Surprisingly, it is François de Menil, who is in his early 50s and obtained his architectural degree in 1987, who came to design the chapel. When asked why she chose her son for this delicate task, Dominique de Menil answers, "I did not commission my son. He saw I was going to build an absurd replica of the original chapel and asked permission to work on a design, which took him almost two years. Its beauty comes from the harmony between concept and execution. I like the material he has chosen. The frosted glass, luminous and a bit immaterial, is a fabulous choice."[7]

A simple palette of materials including precast concrete panels for the exterior, and black slate floors within, highlight the frescoes, suspended on frosted glass and located much as they

Seltsamerweise sind jedoch einige der inspirierendsten Erzeugnisse der Gegenwartsarchitektur gerade mit der Tradition einer religiösen Andacht verbunden, wenn auch oft in einem ökumenischen oder sogar konfessionslosen Zusammenhang. Die Architekten Tadao Ando in Japan und Mario Botta in Europa haben kleine Kapellen geschaffen, die eine Form des religiösen Ausdrucks darstellen, dessen Kraft und Ausstrahlung nicht zu leugnen ist.

Steven Holl, 1947 in Bremerton, Washington, geboren, arbeitet derzeit an der Fertigstellung des Museums für zeitgenössische Kunst in Helsinki. Die gedankliche und ästhetische Subtilität seiner Gestaltung unterscheidet ihn von vielen seiner heute tätigen amerikanischen Architektenkollegen. Holl ist der Typ Architekt, der eher theoretisch veranlagt ist und er hat bewiesen, daß er fähig ist, seine Architektur extrem begrenzten Budgets anzupassen. Ein Beispiel hierfür ist die Jesuitenkapelle, die er vor kurzem für die Seattle University gebaut hat. »Ursprünglich waren wir eins von mehreren an die Seattle University eingeladenen Architekturbüros, die für dieses Projekt in Betracht gezogen wurden«, sagt Holl. »Fünf erreichen die letzte Runde, und jeder von uns mußte an der Universität einen öffentlichen Vortrag halten. Zu Beginn meines Vortrags sagte ich, ich sei zwar kein Katholik, glaube aber fest an die Kraft und Fähigkeit der Architektur, einen religiösen Raum zu schaffen. Ich gab auch zu, daß ich noch nie eine Kapelle gebaut hatte.«[5] Steven Holl gestaltete die Kapelle mit einer Anzahl relativ einfacher Formen sowie mit Licht und ließ sich dabei von den Strukturen des jesuitischen Credos inspirieren. »Die Licht-Metaphern«, so Holl, »in unterschiedlichen Volumen dargestellt, sind aus dem Dach abgeleitet, dessen unregelmäßige Konfiguration verschiedene Lichtqualitäten erzeugen soll. Der Entwurfsgedanke geht vom Einfangen verschiedener Lichtarten aus, wie es in der Konzeptskizze lichtgefüllter Flaschen, die aus einem Steinkasten herauskommen (s. S. 91), ersichtlich wird. Die Jesuiten schreiben nicht nur eine einzige Methode geistlicher Übungen vor, und deshalb wird hier in der Kapelle die Einheit der unterschiedlichen Elemente zu einem Ganzen zusammen-

lité à la fois intellectuelle et esthétique de son approche le distingue de celle de très nombreux architectes américains actuels. C'est un architecte «pensant», qui a prouvé sa capacité à adapter son travail à des contraintes budgétaires extrêmement strictes. La chapelle des Jésuites récemment achevée pour l'Université de Seattle illustre sa démarche. «Au départ, plusieurs architectes avaient été invités par l'Université à réfléchir à ce projet», explique-t-il, «il y eut cinq finalistes, et chacun d'entre nous dû donner une conférence publique à l'Université. Au début de mon intervention, j'ai précisé que je n'étais pas catholique, mais que je croyais fermement à la capacité de l'architecture de créer un espace religieux. J'ai bien sûr avoué que je n'avais jamais construit d'église auparavant.»[5] Utilisant un vocabulaire formel relativement simple, jouant de la lumière, il s'est inspiré de la nature même de la foi jésuitique. «La métaphore de la lumière est mise en forme dans des volumes divers qui émergent du toit et produisent différentes qualités d'éclairage. Le concept est illustré par un dessin d'intention représentant des «bouteilles de lumière» émergeant d'une boîte de pierre (voir page 91). De même qu'il n'existe pas de règle unique pour les exercices spirituels des jésuites, ici, c'est un ensemble de différences qui est réuni pour former un tout. Chacun de ces volumes de lumière correspond à une partie du programme de la liturgie catholique. La lumière du sud symbolise la procession, élément fondamental de la messe. La lumière du nord, face à la ville, éclaire la chapelle du Saint Sacrement et matérialise la mission de dépassement de la communauté.»[6]

Steven Holl a apporté des solutions originales aux nombreuses contraintes budgétaires imposées: «Aucun budget n'avait été prévu pour des vitraux. Nous avons néanmoins construit une série de plans colorés peints par derrière, et inséré un morceau de vitrail de couleur complémentaire au milieu de chacun.» Une technique similaire a été utilisée par l'architecte dans ses bureaux pour D. E. Shaw and Company (New York, NY, 1991). Au lieu de murs de pierre, bien trop coûteux, c'est un béton tilt-up qui a été employé, «exactement comme dans la maison de Schindler pour King's Road».

were in the original chapel, whose form is outlined by steel pipes and more frosted glass. Consecrated as "a living place of worship," the chapel is quite rightly seen by its architect as "a refuge from the chaos that surrounds us," a notion very much akin to the powerful spirit of Tadao Ando's concrete chapels, which may at very least have provided a point of reference in this case. Menil, like Ando, has opted for an austere, geometric concrete exterior. Evoking the history of the objects contained within by the outlined form of the original structure, this chapel too plays on light and dark, giving the frescoes a home that is truly propitious to their viewing and conservation.

Urban Layering

Los Angeles has been a fertile ground for architectural experimentation for some years, giving rise to such internationally recognized talents as that of Frank O. Gehry. As much as it is a place, Los Angeles is a state of mind and a climate that have engendered conditions unlike those encountered by architects anywhere else. It is to some extent coincidental that two talented architects have been working in recent years in and around Culver City, the former home of the movie industry, located between downtown Los Angeles and the ocean. But Culver City, with its vast areas of nearly abandoned warehouses and industrial buildings, is also a fertile ground for experimentation and rehabilitation. The first of these architects is Steven Ehrlich, who was born in 1946 in New Jersey. Unexpectedly, he studied indigenous vernacular architecture in North and West Africa from 1969 to 1977, and taught for three years at Ahmadu Bello University in Zaria, Nigeria. In 1995, he completed the Game Show Network in Culver City, a transformation of 1930s vintage garage into home for the first all-digital cable network. Nearby, his Child Care Center (1992–95) for Sony employees participates in an innovative effort to bring the often deserted streets of Culver City back to life. More recently, Steven Ehrlich designed the Robertson Branch Library, which is located on Robertson Boulevard, a ten minute drive from Culver City. As even the casual visitor to Los Angeles knows, most people in this vast city move around in

gefaßt. Jeder Lichtraum entspricht einem Teil der katholischen Meßliturgie. Das nach Süden gerichtete Licht entspricht der Prozession, einem grundlegenden Bestandteil der Messe. Das Nordlicht zur Stadt hin entspricht der Kapelle des Heiligen Sakraments und der Aussendung der Gläubigen in die Welt.«[6]

Steven Holl fand hier trotz begrenzter Finanzen originelle Lösungen. Er erklärt: »Im Budget waren Buntglasfenster nicht vorgesehen. Wir schufen mehrere Farbfelder mit hintermalten Ablenkblechen und setzten eine einzige Scheibe Buntglas in einer Komplementärfarbe in die Mitte jedes Feldes.« Ähnlich nutzte Holl eine Ersatztechnik bei seinem Bürobau für D.E. Shaw and Company (New York, NY, 1991). Anstelle der zu teuren Natursteinwände setzte er aufwärts geneigte Betonblöcke ein, »genau wie bei Schindlers King's Road House«.

Die Byzantine Chapel von François de Menil in Houston hat einen ganz anderen Ausgangspunkt als Holls Jesuiten-Kapelle im Staat Washington. De Menils Mutter Dominique gehört zu den bekanntesten Kunstmäzenen in den USA und in Europa. Es ist zum großen Teil ihr zu verdanken, daß die berühmte Rothko Chapel von Philip Johnson und die Menil Collection sowie in jüngerer Zeit der Cy Twombly-Pavillon (beide von Renzo Piano) im Stadtteil Montrose von Houston, Texas, gebaut wurden. 1983 interessierte sich Dominique de Menil für zwei byzantinische Fresken aus dem 13. Jahrhundert, die aus einer kleinen Kirche in einem umkämpften Gebiet in Zypern entfernt worden waren. Nachdem sie die Fresken hatte restaurieren lassen, kam die Menil Foundation zu einer Übereinkunft mit dem griechisch-orthodoxen Bistum von Zypern, nach der die Kunstwerke als Dauerleihgabe nach Houston geschafft werden durften, zumindest so lange, bis die Lage in Zypern ihre Rückkehr erlauben sollte. Die Menil Foundation bewies ihren sensiblen Umgang mit gefährdeten Kunstobjekten, indem sie die zur Unterbringung der Fresken gebaute Kapelle und das Baugelände der griechisch-orthodoxen Kirche zur Verfügung stellte. Überraschenderweise war es François de Menil, der Anfang 50 ist und sein Architekturdiplom 1987 erhielt, der die Kapelle entwarf. Als Dominique de Menil gefragt wurde, warum sie ihren Sohn

La chapelle byzantine érigée par François de Menil à Houston part d'un point de vue très différent. Sa mère, Dominique de Menil, est l'un des plus célèbres mécènes des arts aussi bien en Europe qu'aux États-Unis. C'est en grande partie grâce à elle que la fameuse chapelle de Rothko (Philip Johnson), le Musée de la collection Menil, et plus récemment la Cy Twombly Gallery (deux réalisations de Renzo Piano) ont été édifiés dans le quartier de Montrose, à Houston. Dès 1983, Dominique de Menil s'est intéressée au sort de deux fresques byzantines du XIIIe siècle, sauvées d'une chapelle située dans une zone disputée de Chypre. Après avoir fait restaurer ces peintures, la Menil Foundation parvint à un accord avec l'évêché grec orthodoxe chypriote pour que les œuvres soient confiées en dépôt à long terme à Houston, au moins jusqu'à ce que la situation politique chypriote permette leur retour. Pour marquer la sensibilité de la Fondation au destin des œuvres d'art, la chapelle construite pour les abriter et son terrain ont été offerts à l'église orthodoxe grecque. François de Menil, architecte d'une cinquantaine d'années qui a obtenu son diplôme en 1987, a été retenu pour concevoir ce lieu. À la question sur les raisons du choix de son fils, Dominique de Menil répond: «Je n'ai pas passé une commande à mon fils. Il a vu que j'allais construire une copie absurde de la chapelle d'origine et m'a demandé la permission de travailler sur ce projet qui lui a demandé presque deux ans de mise au point. Sa beauté vient de l'harmonie entre le concept et l'exécution. J'aime le matériau qu'il a choisi. Le verre givré, lumineux et légèrement immatériel est un choix fabuleux.»[7]

Une palette de matériaux simples, dont des panneaux de béton préfabriqués pour l'extérieur et un sol en ardoise noire à l'intérieur, mettent en valeur ces fresques suspendues sur des fonds de verre givré à peu près dans la même position où elles se trouvaient à l'origine. L'architecture est évoquée par des tuyaux d'acier et d'autres panneaux de verre. «Lieu de prière vivant», la chapelle est considérée par l'architecte comme «un refuge dans le chaos qui nous entoure», une préoccupation assez proche de celle de Tadao Ando pour ses chapelles en béton qui ont pu servir de référence. Évoquant l'histoire des fresques

Steven Ehrlich, Robertson Branch Library, Los Angeles, California, 1993–97. A simple structure pierced by a copper-clad volume "shaped like the hull of a boat."

Steven Ehrlich, Robertson Branch Library, Los Angeles, Kalifornien, 1993–97. Ein schlichter Baukörper, durchbohrt von einem kupferverkleideten Bauteil »in Form eines Schiffsrumpfes«.

Steven Ehrlich, Robertson Branch Library, Los Angeles, Californie, 1993–97. Construction simple percée par un volume recouvert de cuivre, «en forme de quille de navire».

Steven Ehrlich, Robertson Branch Library, Los Angeles, California, 1993–97. Like a wedge driven through the building, its central element serves to bring light into the reading areas.

Steven Ehrlich, Robertson Branch Library, Los Angeles, Kalifornien, 1993–97. Das zentrale Bauelement, wie ein Keil in das Gebäude hineingetrieben, bringt Tageslicht in die Lesesäle.

Steven Ehrlich, Robertson Branch Library, Los Angeles, Californie, 1993–97. Tel un coin forcé dans le bâtiment, cet élément central a pour fonction l'éclairage des zones de lecture.

cars, and to be noticed, architecture must address itself to that form of transportation. Ehrlich's own firm statement defines the importance of this factor in his design. In this "chaotic urban environment," the architect felt "it was necessary to welcome and to announce the importance of the library both to the community and to the casual passerby." A bold element shaped like the hull of a boat soars above the otherwise modest two-story structure and breaks the monotony of the building's rectangular footprint. This element acts as a marketing device to increase public interest, and ultimately attendance, which has been a city concern as use has diminished in recent years. Clad in copper inside and out, this volume extends through the building and serves as a marquee for the library. Working in collaboration with artist Erika Rothernberg, Ehrlich uses it as a billboard for witticism and pith literary quotations to reaffirm the importance and presence of the public library. A further indication of the importance of the automobile in Los Angeles is the fact that this modestly sized building (about 1,000 square meters) is elevated to allow for the driveway and parking at ground level. Geared to the ephemeral nature of much Los Angeles architecture, the Robertson Branch Library succeeds nonetheless in affirming the perennial nature of the book. Where automobiles rule, Ehrlich has chosen the metaphor of the boat, somehow more solid and more indicative of the kind of intellectual voyage offered to the readers within.

The presence of Eric Owen Moss in Culver City would seem to have a more profound significance than that of Ehrlich or other architects who have worked on individual structures, whether to rehabilitate them, or to build anew. For the past eleven years, Moss has been working almost exclusively with the developers Frederick and Laurie Samitaur Smith, renovating over 30,000 square meters of office space in a 30 hectare district called the Hayden Tract. Ultimately, in the mind of the architect, and of the developers, the goal is to create a new city within the old one. Moss speaks in terms of a "megastructure" that he has called the Southern Pacific Air Rights City. The most recent addition to this ongoing project is the Prittard & Sullivan Building, located

mit dieser heiklen Aufgabe betraute, antwortete sie: »Ich habe meinen Sohn nicht beauftragt. Er bekam mit, daß ich eine absurde Replik der echten zypriotischen Kirche hier bauen lassen wollte und bat um Erlaubnis, selber einen Entwurf zu erarbeiten, wofür er fast zwei Jahre brauchte. Die Schönheit des Neubaus beruht auf der Harmonie zwischen Entwurfsgestaltung und Bauausführung. Mir gefällt das Material, das er ausgesucht hat. Das matte Milchglas, leuchtend und ein bißchen vergeistigt, ist eine wunderbare Wahl.«[7]

Wenige einfache Materialien, einschließlich vorgefertigte Betonpaneele für die Fassaden und schwarzer Schiefer für den Fußboden, bringen die Fresken zur Geltung, die vor das Milchglas gehängt sind. Diese sind ziemlich genauso plaziert wie in der alten Kapelle in Zypern, deren Form mit einem Stahlrohr- skelett und weiteren Milchglaselementen angedeutet wird. Die Kapelle wurde zum »lebendigen Gottesdienstraum« geweiht und vom Architekten treffend »eine Zuflucht vor dem Chaos, das uns umgibt« genannt. Diese Vorstellung entspricht der ein- drucksvollen geistigen Ausstrahlung von Tadao Andos Beton- kapellen, die hier zumindest Bezugspunkte abgegeben haben. Menil hat sich – wie Ando – für schmucklose, geometrisch gegliederte Außenfassaden aus Beton entschieden. Indem sie die Geschichte der in ihr enthaltenen Kunstwerke in den Um- rissen ihrer ursprünglichen Behausung darstellt, spielt auch diese Kapelle mit Licht und Dunkelheit und gibt den Fresken eine Heimstatt, die wirklich günstige Bedingungen für ihre Be- trachtung und Erhaltung bietet.

Stadt-Schichtungen

Los Angeles ist seit einigen Jahren fruchtbarer Boden für archi- tektonische Experimente und hat so international anerkannte Talente gefördert wie Frank O. Gehry. Los Angeles ist nicht nur eine Stadt, sondern steht ebenso für eine Geisteshaltung wie für ein Klima, die Bedingungen entstehen ließen, wie sie sich Architekten nirgendwo sonst bieten. Bis zu einem gewissen Grad ist es Zufall, daß zwei hervorragende Architekten in den letzten Jahren in und um Culver City gebaut haben, der früheren

par une reconstitution virtuelle de la chapelle d'origine, cette construction joue avec l'ombre et la lumière. Elle offre à ces œuvres une demeure réellement conçue pour leur exposition et leur conservation.

Strates urbaines

Depuis quelques années, Los Angeles est un terrain d'expéri- mentation architecturale fertile. C'est ici que sont apparus des talents aujourd'hui reconnus dans le monde entier, comme Frank O. Gehry. L. A. est une ville, mais aussi un état d'esprit et un climat qui ont engendré un contexte différent de celui que connaissent les architectes en général. C'est dans une certaine mesure une coïncidence si deux architectes de talent se sont retrouvés à travailler récemment dans et autour de Culver City, ancien bastion de l'industrie cinématographique, situé entre le centre de Los Angeles et l'océan. Culver City avec ses immenses zones d'entrepôts et de bâtiments industriels quasi abandonnés est également un extraordinaire champ d'expérimentations et de réhabilitation. Le premier de ces architectes est Steven Ehrlich, né en 1946 dans le New Jersey. Après son diplôme, il a étudié l'architecture vernaculaire indigène en Afrique du Nord et de l'Ouest de 1969 à 1977, et enseigné pendant trois ans à Ahmadu Bello University à Zaria, au Nigeria. En 1995, il a achevé le Game Show Network à Culver City, reconversion d'un garage des années 30 en siège social du premier réseau de télévision câblée numérique. Tout près, son Child Care Center (1992–95) pour le personnel de Sony, participe à l'effort de rénovation qui veut ramener à la vie les rues de Culver City si souvent désertées. Plus récemment, il a dessiné la Robertson Branch Library, située sur Robertson Boulevard, à dix minutes de Culver City. Comme on le sait, la plupart des habitants de Los Angeles ne se déplacent qu'en voiture, et pour être remarquée, l'architecture doit tenir compte de ce moyen de transport qui détermine sa perception. Dans la présentation de son agence, Ehrlich définit l'importance de ce facteur dans son travail. Pour répondre à cet «environ- nement urbain chaotique, il était nécessaire de faire savoir l'importance de cette bibliothèque, et de l'annoncer à la fois à

Eric Owen Moss, Prittard & Sullivan Building, Culver City, California, 1995–97. A sculptural combination of elements from a building formerly on the site with the new structure.

Eric Owen Moss, Prittard & Sullivan-Bau, Culver City, Kalifornien, 1995–97. Eine plastische Komposition aus Alt- und Neubauteilen.

Eric Owen Moss, Prittard & Sullivan Building, Culver City, Californie, 1995–97. Combinaison sculpturale d'éléments appartenant à un bâtiment préexistant et d'une structure nouvelle.

close to other Moss buildings such as Samitaur, or The Box. As he has in other cases, the architect has undertaken a complex process of layering existing buildings and his own reinterpretation, in this case maintaining a central group of wooden posts, trusses and a brick wall from the original bow-string-trussed warehouse. Evoking the idea of "residual memory," Moss says, "Every culture lays their forms on top of what's already there." This seems to be a surprising notion in the context of a city as modern as Los Angeles, but even if its past cannot be traced much beyond the turn of the century, Culver City has already gone through a cycle of construction and abandonment which makes the approach of Moss perfectly valid. More interesting on an intellectual and design level is the fact that Eric Owen Moss has not only taken into account what was and is now on this site, but also what might have been there. He also designed a house and a theater for this location, and their virtual presence is integrated into the final design, the residence becoming the lobby of Prittard & Sullivan. Eccentric and sculptural in many areas, this building is treated over a good part of its surface like a normal office space, rendering it flexible and easy to use. Its sculptural qualities give it a signature style which is that of Eric Owen Moss but also that of the Smiths, and progressively of a new Culver City that is capable of attracting some of the most creative firms in areas such as the music industry. By layering past, present, and future, Moss is pointing the way to a real art of urban renovation, while others like Steven Ehrlich build into this environment in a more classical way, going where their clients and their commissions take them.

New Temples of Art

The wave of museum construction, which reached its height in the 1980s, is meant to have receded, leaving in its wake institutions that are often difficult to finance in the more sober economic climate of the 1990s. Though museum building in most of the developed world is proceeding at a much slower pace than a few years ago, a few notable exceptions seem to deny this rule, perhaps because the projects involved actually got under way in

Heimat der Filmindustrie, die zwischen dem Stadtzentrum von Los Angeles und dem Pazifik liegt. Mit seinen ausgedehnten Komplexen aus fast schon aufgegebenen Lagerhäusern und Industriebauten ist Culver City auch ein fruchtbarer Boden für Experimente sowie für Sanierung und Rekonstruktion. Der erste dieser begabten Architekten ist Steven Ehrlich, 1946 in New Jersey geboren. Man ist überrascht, wenn man hört, daß er von 1969 bis 1977 in Nord- und Westafrika traditionelle afrikanische Architektur und Baumethoden erforscht hat und drei Jahre an der Ahmadu Bello University in Zaria, Nigeria, lehrte. 1995 vollendete er das Game Show Network in Culver City, den Umbau eines alten Garagengebäudes aus den 30er Jahren zum Sitz des ersten voll digitalisierten Kabelsenders. Ehrlichs in der Nähe gelegenes Child Care Center (1992–95) für die Kinder von Sony-Mitarbeitern ist einer von vielen phantasievollen Versuchen, die oft menschenleeren Straßen von Culver City zu neuem Leben zu erwecken. In jüngster Zeit hat Steven Ehrlich die Robertson Branch Library am Robertson Boulevard gebaut, zehn Autominuten von Culver City entfernt. Selbst diejenigen, die sich nur kurz in L.A. aufhalten, wissen, daß die meisten Menschen sich in dieser Stadt per Auto fortbewegen, und Gebäude müssen daher auf die Sicht aus diesem Transportmittel ausgerichtet sein, wenn sie bemerkt werden sollen. Ehrlich selbst hat die Bedeutung dieses Faktors für seine Architekturgestaltung herausgestrichen. In dieser »chaotischen städtischen Umgebung« habe er es für notwenig gehalten, die Bibliothek »sowohl für die Ortsgemeinde als auch den gelegentlichen Passanten willkommen zu heißen und anzukündigen«. Ein kühnes, schiffsrumpfartiges Element erhebt sich hoch über den ansonsten bescheidenen zweistöckigen Bau und unterbricht die Monotonie des rechteckigen Kastens. Es wirkt wie eine Marketing-Maßnahme, d.h. es erregt öffentliche Aufmerksamkeit und lockt auch mehr Bibliotheksbesucher an, was die Sorgen der Stadtbehörden um die in den letzten Jahren zurückgehenden Benutzerzahlen in Hoffnung gekehrt hat. Das innen und außen mit Kupfer verkleidete »Schiff« erstreckt sich durch das ganze Gebäude und bildet auch das Eingangsvordach der Bibliothek. In Zusammenarbeit

la communauté locale et aux passants occasionnels.» Un audacieux élément en forme de quille de navire se dresse au-dessus d'une structure de deux niveaux, par ailleurs modeste, et rompt la monotonie de l'empreinte rectangulaire du bâtiment. Cet élément agit comme un procédé de marketing pour attirer l'attention du public, et en dernier ressort augmenter la fréquentation des lecteurs qui avait diminué au cours des années récentes. Plaqué de cuivre, aussi bien à l'extérieur qu'à l'intérieur, ce volume se développe à travers le bâtiment et sert d'auvent dans la bibliothèque. En collaboration avec l'artiste Erika Rothernberg, Ehrlich a créé un panneau d'affichage de citations littéraires provocantes ou amusantes qui réaffirme «l'importance et la présence de la bibliothèque publique». Une preuve supplémentaire de l'importance de l'automobile à Los Angeles est donnée par la surélévation de cette construction de taille réduite (environ 1 000 m²) pour permettre l'accès des automobiles et le stationnement au niveau du sol. Adaptée à la nature éphémère de la plupart des réalisations architecturales de Los Angeles, la Robertson Branch Library réussit néanmoins à affirmer la pérennité de l'écrit. Là où règne l'automobile, Ehrlich a choisi la métaphore du bateau, d'une certaine façon plus pertinente pour traduire le type de voyage intellectuel offert aux usagers à l'intérieur.

La présence d'Eric Owen Moss à Culver City semble revêtir un sens plus profond que celle d'Ehrlich ou d'autres architectes qui ont travaillé sur des réalisations dans ce quartier, que ce soit pour les réhabiliter ou construire à neuf. Au cours de ces onze dernières années, Moss a travaillé presque exclusivement pour les promoteurs Frederick et Laurie Samitaur Smith, et a rénové près de 30 000 m² de bureaux dans un secteur de 30 hectares appelé le Hayden Tract. En fait, dans l'esprit de l'architecte et des promoteurs, il s'agit de créer ici une ville nouvelle au cœur de l'ancienne. Moss parle d'ailleurs d'une «mégastructure» qu'il appelle la «Southern Pacific Air Rights City». Le plus récent ajout à ce projet en cours de développement est le Prittard & Sullivan Building, situé à proximité d'autres réalisations de Moss, tels Samitaur ou The Box. Comme il l'a fait à d'autres occasions,

more optimistic times. This is certainly the case for Richard Meier's massive Getty Center, located on a magnificent hilltop in Brentwood, an area of Los Angeles. This 88,000 square meter six-building complex situated on a 44.5 hectare site got underway in 1984. Its survival in much the original form through the complicated design and construction phases is a testimony to the financial and intellectual wherewithal of the Getty Trust, whose substantial funding must under California law be spent at a regular and high pace. Unexpectedly, the Getty Center is in many ways unlike anything else Richard Meier has designed, including his more recent Rachofsky House, included in this volume. In the place of the white metallic surfaces of which the architect is so fond, here there is often an off-white, or even beige tone in the cladding. Most remarkable is the extensive use of a heavy cleft travertine, which gives an almost ancient appearance to this once in a lifetime commission. "In my mind's eye," said Richard Meier in 1995, "I see a classic structure, elegant and timeless, emerging, serene and ideal, from the rough hillside, a kind of Artistotelian structure within the landscape. Sometimes I think that the landscape overtakes it, and sometime I see the structure as standing out, dominating the landscape; the two are entwined in a dialogue, a perpetual embrace in which building and site are one. In my mind I keep returning to the Romans – to Hadrian's Villa, to Caprarola for their sequence of spaces, their thick-walled presence, their sense of order, the way in which building and landscape belong to each other." The reference to Caprarola, the Palazzo Farnèse, built by Giacomo da Vignola (1507–73), near Viterbo in 1559, is particularly unexpected. The very rare pentagonal plan of this castle, laden with occult symbolism, and its rather forbidding exterior, dominating the town, seem quite distant from the grace and light of Meier's finest works. The reference to Hadrian's Villa with its complex, off-axis alignments is readily detectable in the Getty complex. Even the museum is conceived not as a continuous block, but as a series of pavilions, which are stepped around a partially open internal courtyard space. With its luxuriant vegetation, its numerous convivial outdoor spaces and its viewpoints toward the city and the ocean,

mit der Künstlerin Erika Rothernberg nutzte Ehrlich es als Anschlagtafel für geistreiche Bonmots und prägnante Literaturzitate, um die Bedeutung und Präsenz der öffentlichen Bibliothek zu betonen. Ein weiteres Anzeichen für die Wichtigkeit des Autos in Los Angeles ist die Tatsache, daß dieses bescheiden dimensionierte Gebäude (ca. 1 000 m² Fläche) aufgeständert ist, damit Zufahrt und Parkplätze auf Straßenniveau eingerichtet werden konnten. Die Robertson Branch Library entspricht zwar der sozusagen ephemeren Architektur von Los Angeles, bestätigt zugleich aber das dauerhafte Wesen des Buches. Wo das Auto regiert, setzt Ehrlich die Metapher des Schiffs ein, das irgendwie solider ist und ein besseres Symbol für die intellektuellen Reisen, die den Lesern im Innern geboten werden.

Die Präsenz von Eric Owen Moss in Culver City ist vielleicht bedeutender als die Bautätigkeit Ehrlichs oder anderer Architekten, die einzelne Projekte – entweder Um- oder Neubauten – dort realisiert haben. In den letzten elf Jahren hat Moss fast ausschließlich für die Investoren Frederick und Laurie Samitaur Smith gearbeitet. Er modernisierte in dem 30 Hektar großen Stadtgebiet Hayden Tract über 30 000 m² Büros, letztlich mit dem Ziel, innerhalb der alten eine neue Stadt zu schaffen. Moss spricht hier von einer »Megastruktur«, die er »Southern Pacific Air Rights City« nennt. In dieser im Aufbau begriffenen Neustadt stellt das Prittard & Sullivan Gebäude in der Nähe der anderen Moss-Bauten (Samitaur, The Box) den letzten Neuzugang dar. Wie andernorts hat der Architekt hier vorhandene Bauteile mit eigenen Eingriffen vielfältig vermischt und geschichtet, wobei er eine zentrale Gruppe von Holzpfeilern, Trägern und eine Ziegelmauer von der zugverspannten Bogenträgerkonstruktion des alten Lagerhauses übernahm. Moss spricht von »Resterinnerung« und sagt: »Jede Kultur überlagert Vorhandenes mit ihren eigenen Formen«. Das scheint in einer so modernen Stadt wie Los Angeles eine überraschende Vorstellung zu sein, aber selbst wenn die Stadtgeschichte nicht sehr weit über die Jahrhundertwende zurückreicht, hat Culver City bereits einen Zyklus von Aufbau, Abriß und Neubau hinter sich, der Moss' Ansatz rechtfertigt. Auf inhaltlicher und gestalterischer Ebene ist

*Richard Meier, Getty Center, Los Angeles, California,
1984–97. An overall view of the Brentwood hilltop
where the Getty Center is located.*

*Richard Meier, Getty Center, Los Angeles, Kalifornien,
1984–97. Gesamtansicht der Hügelkuppe in Brentwood,
Standort des Getty Center.*

*Richard Meier, Getty Center, Los Angeles, Californie,
1984–97. Vue générale du sommet de la colline
de Brentwood sur laquelle s'élève le Getty Center.*

Richard Meier, Getty Center, Los Angeles, California,
1984–97. The arrival point of the tramway which brings
visitors near the entrance to the J. Paul Getty Museum.

Richard Meier, Getty Center, Los Angeles, Kalifornien,
1984–97. Haltestelle der Straßenbahn, die Besucher
bis nahe an den Eingang zum J. Paul Getty Museum
heranführt.

Richard Meier, Getty Center, Los Angeles, Californie,
1984–97. Gare du tramway qui conduit les visiteurs à
l'entrée du J. Paul Getty Museum.

the Getty Center does make a connection with the California
lifestyle, but it also speaks of Italy, where so much of architectural
history was written. It could certainly be said that with the
Getty project, Richard Meier, one of the most fervent admirers
of the Modernist tradition, has confirmed the shift of modern
architecture, art, and design to a mode more specifically open
to the past. By no means reactionary, perhaps even less so
than in his purest white creations, Meier stakes his claim on
this Brentwood hillside to a real place in the history of his art,
intimately linked to the past and prepared for the future.

If Richard Meier's Getty Center has been likened to a monastery,
sitting on its Los Angeles hilltop, so others have compared the
new museums to modern cathedrals. As the noted critic of Postmodernism, Charles Jencks wrote about Frank O. Gehry's new
Guggenheim Museum Bilbao: "Rarely does a building capture
the imagination of both architects and the public. Le Corbusier's
Ronchamp and Utzon's Sydney Opera House did in the Sixties
and Seventies and now Frank O. Gehry's Guggenheim Museum,
in the Basque city of Bilbao, becomes another of these rare
events... one is reminded of Chartres cathedral proclaiming itself
in the landscape and the city... Coincidentally, it also epitomizes
a trend which has been under way for thirty years – the museum
as cathedral."[8] Located in the center of the cultural district
formed by the Museo de Bellas Artes, the University de Deusto,
and the Opera House, on a 32,700 square meter site formerly
occupied by a factory and parking lot, the new Bilbao Museum
opened in mid-October 1997. Three architects participated
in an invited competition, Gehry, Arata Isozaki, and Coop
Himmelb(l)au, and the groundbreaking took place on October
22, 1993. Designed in a cooperative arrangement with New
York's Guggenheim, the museum has 10,500 square meters of
galleries, 2,500 square meters of public space, with a 50 meter
high atrium, an auditorium, a museum store, a restaurant,
and a café. Project cost for the 24,000 square meter building
was estimated at $100 million. A sculptural metallic roof form
reminiscent of a " metallic flower," designed with the assistance
of the CATIA three-dimensional aerospace computer modeling

interessant, daß Moss nicht nur berücksichtigt hat, was früher
auf dem Grundstück war und heute noch ist, sondern auch das,
was hätte sein können. Er hatte schon einmal ein Wohnhaus
und ein Theater für dieses Grundstück entworfen und nun deren
virtuelle Gegenwart in den endgültigen Entwurf integriert, wobei
das Wohnhaus die Eingangshalle des Firmengebäudes von
Prittard & Sullivan bildet. Der Bau ist an vielen Stellen exzentrisch
und plastisch ausgeformt, andererseits aber zum großen Teil
wie ein normales Bürohaus durchgestaltet, flexibel und nutzer-
freundlich. Seine plastische Qualität kennzeichnet es als Werk
von Moss, ebenso als Bau der Smiths – und schließlich als
typisch für die neue Culver City, die zum Anziehungspunkt
für einige der kreativsten Firmen, zum Beispiel des Musik-
geschäftes, geworden ist. Indem er Historisches, Gegenwärtiges
und Zukunftsweisendes überlagert, zeigt Moss den Weg zur
wahren Kunst städtebaulicher Erneuerung, während andere
wie Steven Ehrlich in eher klassischer Weise in diesen Kontext
eingreifen, indem sie sich dort bewegen, wo ihre Bauherren und
Aufträge sie hinführen.

Neue Kunsttempel
Die Welle von Museumsbauten erreichte ihren Höhepunkt in
den 8oer Jahren. Jetzt ist sie im Abflauen begriffen und hinterläßt
Bauten, deren Betrieb im ernüchterten Wirtschaftsklima der
90er schwieriger zu finanzieren ist. Richard Meiers Getty Center
wurde in herrlicher Lage auf einem Hügel in Brentwood,
Los Angeles, errichtet. Mit der Planung des Zentrums (sechs
Gebäude mit einer Gesamtfläche von 88 000 m² auf einem
44,5 Hektar großen Gelände) wurde 1984 begonnen. Daß es den
komplizierten Entwurfs- und Bauprozeß zum größten Teil
in der ursprünglich vorgesehenen Form überlebte, belegt die
finanziellen und intellektuellen Möglichkeiten des Getty Trust,
der nach kalifornischem Gesetz seine Fördermittel und Spenden
kontinuierlich in großen Summen ausgeben muß. Überraschenderweise ist das Getty Center in vielerlei Hinsicht anders als alle
anderen Bauten von Richard Meier, einschließlich des Hauses
Rachofsky. Anstelle der von Meier bevorzugten reinweißen

avec des investissements plus modestes que précedemment,
quelques exceptions notables démentent cette règle, sans doute
parce que ces projets ont été lancés au cours d'une période plus
optimiste. C'est certainement le cas de l'énorme Getty Center de
Richard Meier, érigé dans un site magnifique au sommet d'une
colline de Brentwood, à Los Angeles. L'édification de ce complexe
de six bâtiments totalisant 88 000 m² sur 44,5 hectares de terrain
a été entreprise en 1984. Le respect pour l'essentiel des plans
originaux témoigne du soutien financier et intellectuel résolu du
Getty Trust, dont les revenus abondants doivent être dépensés à
un rythme élevé pour respecter la réglementation californienne.
Curieusement, le Getty Center est à de multiples égards différent
de tout ce que Richard Meier a conçu jusque là, y compris
sa récente Rachofsky House, présentée par ailleurs dans cet
ouvrage. À la place des surfaces métalliques blanches dont
l'architecte est si friand, on trouve ici souvent un parement en
pierre blanc cassé ou même beige. Plus remarquable cependant
est le recours omniprésent à un travertin rugueux qui donne
une apparence presque ancienne à cette réalisation d'une
importance telle qu'un architecte ne peut en recevoir qu'une
dans sa vie. «Dans mon esprit», précisait Richard Meier en 1995,
«je vois une structure classique, élégante et intemporelle,
émergeant, sereine et idéale, du flanc sauvage de la colline,
sorte de structure aristotélicienne dans le paysage. Parfois, je
pense que le paysage la domine, à d'autres moments, je la vois se
dresser dominant son environnement. Tous deux sont engagés
dans un dialogue, un enlacement dans lequel le bâtiment et le
site ne font qu'un. Dans mon esprit, je ne cesse de revenir aux
Romains, à la villa d'Hadrien, à Caprarola, pour leur succession
d'espaces, la forte présence des murs, le sens de l'ordre, la
manière dont le bâtiment et le paysage appartiennent l'un à
l'autre.» La référence à Caprarola, le Palais Farnèse construit
par Giacomo da Vignola (1507–73) près de Viterbe en 1559, est
particulièrement inattendue. Le plan pentagonal très rare de ce
château dominant la ville, chargé d'un symbolisme occulte, et
son aspect extérieur assez terrifiant semblent plutôt éloignés de
la grâce et de la légèreté des œuvres les plus raffinées de Meier.

program, unifies the project into a single architectural composition. Building materials are titanium, limestone, and glass. The museum's largest space is a large boat-shaped gallery completely free of structural columns and measuring 130 meters by 30 meters. Most gallery ceiling heights are 6 meters or more, which together with the spectacular atrium, gives a feeling of space akin only to cathedrals. Coupled with a new subway line designed by Sir Norman Foster, and a bridge and airport by Santiago Calatrava, the Guggenheim Bilbao announces the faith of the city, region and Spanish government in the renewal of this industrial city through the force of contemporary architecture and design. Just as great cathedrals in the past often proclaimed the wealth and power of the cities in which they were located, so the museums and other culturally oriented projects of today stake similar claims. It of course remains to be seen if these strong signals are enough to transform public opinion or to modify the very fabric of a city's activities. In any case, the authorities of Bilbao have not gone about this project in a modest way. They have invested heavily, and the results they obtain may well have an impact on the future development of cities throughout the world.

A comparison of Meier's Getty Center and Gehry's Guggenheim Bilbao reveals two very different types of architecture, one of stone, rooted in a Mediterranean tradition, another of metal, expressionist and sculptural in its development. Both are the results of unique circumstances, not likely to be repeated or even approached in the years to come. Economic conditions and the creativity of contemporary architecture in general would seem to indicate that these two buildings may come to be considered as being the high points of the inventiveness of American architects in the post-War period. Aesthetically situated at almost diametrical opposites, they are evidence of the fundamental lack of any *zeitgeist* beyond that which dictates that art is worthy of the highest praise and efforts. A time that glorifies art may not be as bad as many seem to think.

In many ways, one of the most exceptional and unusual projects to be presented in this book is I.M. Pei's Miho Museum,

Metallverkleidungen wurden hier gebrochen weiße bzw. beigefarbene Materialien gewählt. Am auffälligsten sind die Fassadenteile aus massivem ungeschliffenen Travertin, der diesem im Leben eines Architekten einzigartigen Bauwerk eine fast antike Wirkung verleiht. 1995 sagte Richard Meier: »Vor meinem inneren Auge sehe ich einen klassischen Bau, elegant und zeitlos, der sich heiter und in idealer Form aus dem felsigen Abhang erhebt, eine Art aristotelischer Konstruktion in der Landschaft. Manchmal denke ich, daß diese den Bau überholt, manchmal sehe ich ihn als herausragend, d.h. die Landschaft dominierend. Sie halten Zwiesprache miteinander, halten sich dauerhaft umschlungen. Gebäude und Gelände bilden eine Einheit. In Gedanken kehre ich immer wieder zu den Bauten der Römer zurück, zur Hadriansvilla oder nach Caprarola, und zwar wegen ihrer Raumfolgen, ihrer dickwandigen Präsenz, ihrem Gespür für Ordnungen, wegen der Art und Weise, in der Architektur und Landschaft eins sind.« Die Bezugnahme auf Caprarola, d.h. den 1559 von Giacomo Barozzi, genannt Vignola (1507–73), in der Nähe von Viterbo erbauten Palazzo Farnese, ist besonders unerwartet. Der sehr seltene pentagonale Plan des Palazzos – voller geheimnisvoller Symbolik – und sein ziemlich abweisendes Äußeres, das den Ort dominiert, scheinen weit entfernt von der Eleganz und dem Licht von Meiers besten Bauten. Der Bezug zur Hadriansvilla mit ihrer komplexen, aus der Achse verschobenen Gliederung ist dagegen im Getty Komplex leicht zu entdecken. Selbst das Museum ist kein geschlossener Block, sondern besteht aus einer Reihe von Pavillons unterschiedlicher Höhe, die um einen teilweise offenen Innenhof gruppiert sind. Mit seiner üppigen Vegetation, zahlreichen angenehmen Aufenthaltsbereichen im Freien und Ausblicken auf die Stadt und den Pazifik ist das Getty Center eng mit dem kalifornischen Lebensstil verbunden, erinnert aber auch an Italien, wo große Teile unserer Architekturgeschichte geschrieben wurden. Auf jeden Fall kann man sagen, daß Richard Meier, einer der größten Bewunderer der klassischen Moderne, den Wechsel der Gegenwartsarchitektur und -kunst sowie des modernen Designs hin zu mehr Offenheit gegenüber den geschichtlichen Gegebenheiten

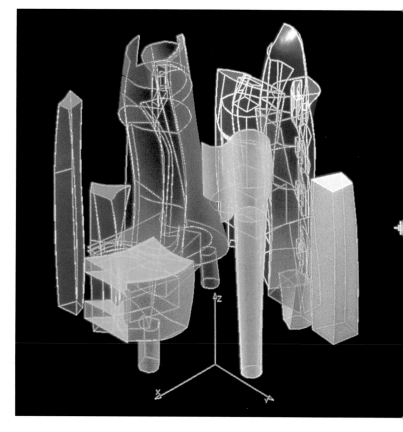

*Frank O. Gehry, Guggenheim Museum Bilbao, Bilbao,
Spain, 1991–97. The architect used the CATIA program
developed by Dassault for aircraft design for this project.*

*Frank O. Gehry, Guggenheim Museum Bilbao, Bilbao,
Spanien, 1991–97. Für die Entwurfsarbeiten nutzte der
Architekt das CATIA-Computerprogramm, das Dassault
für Flugzeugdesign entwickelt hatte.*

*Frank O. Gehry, Musée Guggenheim de Bilbao, Bilbao,
Espagne, 1991–97. L'architecte s'est ici servi du logiciel
CATIA développé par Dassault pour la conception de
ses avions de chasse.*

La référence à la villa d'Hadrien avec ses alignements complexes
et décalés se perçoit mieux dans la complexité du Getty Center.
Le musée lui-même n'est pas conçu comme un bloc continu,
mais comme une série de pavillons qui s'échelonnent autour
d'une cour intérieure en partie ouverte. Avec sa végétation luxu-
riante, ses nombreux espaces extérieurs conviviaux et ses points
de vue vers la ville et l'océan, le Getty Trust, qui appartient in-
contestablement au style de vie californien, parle aussi de l'Italie,
de cette Italie à laquelle l'histoire de l'architecture doit tant.
On peut affirmer qu'avec le projet Getty, Richard Meier, l'un
des plus fervents admirateurs de la tradition moderniste, confirme l'évolution de l'architecture, de l'art et du design actuels
vers des expressions plus ouvertes sur le passé. En aucun cas
réactionnaire, moins encore peut-être que dans ses créations
puristes et blanches, Meier peut prétendre ici, sur cette colline de
Brentwood, à une place de choix dans l'histoire d'une architecture intimement liée au passé et ouverte sur l'avenir.

Si le Getty Center, isolé au sommet de sa colline à Los Angeles,
a pu être comparé à un monastère, d'autres ont vu dans les
nouveaux musées des cathédrales modernes. Comme le célèbre
critique du postmodernisme Charles Jencks l'a écrit au sujet
du nouveau Musée Guggenheim de Bilbao de Frank O. Gehry:
«Il est rare qu'un bâtiment semble capturer à la fois l'imagination des architectes et celle du public. Le Corbusier l'a fait à
Ronchamp, comme Utzon à l'Opéra de Sydney dans les années
60 et 70, et aujourd'hui, Frank O. Gehry y parvient pour
le Musée Guggenheim dans la ville basque de Bilbao... On se
rappelle presque la cathédrale de Chartres se dressant au-dessus
des champs de blé et de la ville... Par coïncidence, le musée
illustre également une tendance qui se dessine depuis 30 ans:
le musée en tant que cathédrale.»[8] Situé au centre d'un secteur
culturel formé par le Museo de Bellas Artes, l'Université de
Deusto et l'Opéra, sur un site de 32 700 m² naguère occupé par
une usine et un parc de stationnement, le nouveau Musée de
Bilbao a été inauguré à la mi-octobre 1997. Trois architectes ont
participé au concours sur invitation: Gehry, Arata Isozaki et
Coop Himmelb(l)au. Le creusement des fondations a débuté le

located in the mountains near Shigaraki in Shiga Prefecture, about one and a half hours from Kyoto by car. Built on a spectacular wooded site located in a nature reserve, the museum must be approached through a tunnel and via a post-tensioned cable bridge, a solution chosen by the architect to avoid disfiguring the landscape as much as possible. Once at the steps leading to the entrance, the visitor can hardly suspect the substantial size of the galleries within, because the building is more than 80% below ground, in order to respect the strict environmental laws of Japan. Both in the steps leading to the door, and in the immediately obvious outline of the roof above, it is clear that an experience much like that involved in visiting a Japanese temple awaits the visitor. Shinji-Shûmeikai, the organization that built the Miho Museum and a Bell Tower completed by Pei in 1990, is dedicated to the pursuit of beauty in nature and art, and the museum in many ways represents a culmination of that search. Both in the remarkable detailing and quality of the architecture, and in the exceptional nature of the archeological objects displayed within, this museum is a unique work of art. Pei employs a stone already used beneath his Louvre Pyramid, and the pyramidal design of the overhead skylights also brings to mind the Parisian museum. Despite these similarities, and the unusual conditions of the commission, which led to expansions and structural changes even as the construction work advanced, I.M. Pei in his eightieth year confirms with the Miho Museum that he is in many respects the greatest of living architects. When seen in the context of his long line of recent major projects, ranging from the Louvre to the Bank of China tower in Hong Kong, and to newer, still unbuilt work, the Miho Museum stands out as a kind of jewel, completed against all likelihood in a remote area of Japan. Delving deeply into the soil and tradition of Japan, the Miho Museum is also designed with Pei's native China in mind. He emphasizes the similarity of the site to Chinese landscapes, and it was a shared familiarity with the Chinese classics that led him to form his excellent relationship with the former head of Shinji-Shûmeikai, Mrs. Mihoko Koyama, a relationship he continued with her daughter, Ms. Hiroko Koyama. The round opening

bestätigt hat. Meier ist dabei durchaus nicht reaktionär (sogar noch weniger als man bei seinen rein-weißen Kreationen annehmen könnte), sondern beansprucht auf dem Hügel in Brentwood seinen Platz in der Geschichte der Architektur – einen Platz für seine Kunst, die so tief mit der Vergangenheit verbunden und auf die Zukunft vorbereitet ist.

Meiers Getty Center ist mit einem Kloster verglichen worden, das auf einem Hügel in Los Angeles sitzt, andere haben die neuen Museumsbauten moderne Kathedralen genannt. Charles Jencks, der bekannte Kritiker der Postmoderne, schrieb folgendes zu Frank O. Gehrys neuem Guggenheim Museum in Bilbao: »Selten fasziniert ein Gebäude sowohl Architekten als auch das allgemeine Publikum. Le Corbusiers Ronchamp-Kapelle und Jørn Utzons Opernhaus in Sydney gelang dies in den Sechzigern und Siebzigern, und Frank O. Gehrys Guggenheim Museum in der baskischen Stadt Bilbao ist eine weitere dieser Seltenheiten... [Es] erinnert an die Kathedrale von Chartres, indem es sich in der Landschaft und in der Stadt behauptet... Zufällig steht es auch für einen Trend, der vor dreißig Jahren einsetzte: das Museum als Kathedrale.«[8] Das neue Museum wurde Mitte Oktober 1997 eröffnet. Es steht im Zentrum des vom Museo de Bellas Artes, der Deusto-Universität und dem Opernhaus gebildeten Kulturviertels auf einem 32 700 m² großen Gelände, auf dem sich vorher eine Fabrik und Parkplätze befanden. Drei Architekturbüros waren zu einem Wettbewerb eingeladen – Gehry, Arata Isozaki und Coop Himmelb(l)au –, und der erste Spatenstich erfolgte am 22. Oktober 1993. Das Museum entstand aufgrund einer Kooperationsvereinbarung mit dem New Yorker Guggenheim und verfügt über 10 500 m² Ausstellungsflächen, 2 500 m² öffentliche Räume, ein 50 m hohes Atrium, ein Auditorium, ein Magazin, ein Restaurant und ein Café. Die Baukosten für insgesamt 24 000 m² Nutzfläche wurden auf 100 Millionen $ geschätzt. Ein plastisch geformtes Dach erinnert an eine »Metallblume«. Die Dachform entstand mit Hilfe des dreidimensional arbeitenden, ursprünglich für die Luft- und Raumfahrt entwickelten Computer-Modellierprogramms CATIA und vereint die einzelnen Teile zu einem geschlossenen architekto-

22 octobre 1993. Conçu en association avec le Musée Guggenheim de New York, le musée possède 10 500 m² de galeries, 2 500 m² d'espaces publics, dont un atrium de 50 m de haut, un auditorium, une boutique, un restaurant et un café. Le coût de construction des 24 000 m² est estimé à 100 millions de \$. Un toit métallique sculptural évoquant une «fleur de métal», conçu à l'aide d'un logiciel de création par ordinateur en trois dimensions, utilisé habituellement en aéronautique, permet l'unité architecturale du projet. Les matériaux utilisés sont le titane, le calcaire et le verre. Le plus vaste espace du musée est une énorme galerie en forme de nef, libre de toute colonne de soutien et mesurant 130 x 30 m. La plupart des plafonds des galeries mesurent 6 m de haut ou plus, ce qui, avec le spectaculaire atrium, donne un sentiment d'espace proche de celui d'une cathédrale. Édifié parallèlement à une nouvelle ligne de métro conçue par Sir Norman Foster, un pont et un aéroport signés Santiago Calatrava, le Musée Guggenheim de Bilbao affirme la foi de la municipalité, de la région et du gouvernement espagnol dans le renouveau de cette cité industrielle par la force de l'effet de l'architecture et du design contemporains. De même que par le passé, les grandes cathédrales témoignant de la puissance et de la richesse de la cité qui les avait construites, les musées et certains autres projets culturels remplissent aujourd'hui une fonction similaire. Il reste à vérifier si ces puissants signaux seront suffisants pour transformer l'opinion publique ou modifier le tissu des activités d'une ville. Il est néanmoins sûr que les autorités de Bilbao se sont totalement engagées dans ce projet. Elles ont investi sans compter, et le résultat de cette opération pourrait bien exercer une influence sur le développement de nombreuses villes à travers le monde.

La comparaison entre le Getty Center de Meier et le Musée Guggenheim de Bilbao de Gehry met en lumière deux types d'architecture différents. L'une est de pierre, enracinée dans une tradition méditerranéenne, l'autre de métal, expressionniste et sculpturale dans son développement. Toutes deux sont nées de circonstances spécifiques, qui ne se retrouveront sans doute jamais réunies dans les années à venir. Les conditions écono-

Frank O. Gehry, Guggenheim Museum Bilbao, Bilbao, Spain, 1991–97. A view of the museum as it can be seen from the opposite bank of the Nervión River in central Bilbao.

Frank O. Gehry, Guggenheim Museum Bilbao, Bilbao, Spanien, 1991–97. Gesamtansicht vom gegenüberliegenden Ufer des Nervión im Stadtzentrum von Bilbao.

Frank O. Gehry, Musée Guggenheim de Bilbao, Bilbao, Espagne, 1991–97. Vue du musée prise de la rive opposée du Nervión, dans le centre de Bilbao.

I.M. Pei, Miho Museum, Shigaraki, Shiga, Japan,
1992–97. Public space in the museum offers a view
toward the surrounding unspoiled countryside.
Pei's Bell Tower, also built for Shinji-Shûmeikai, is
visible in the distance to the left.

I.M. Pei, Miho Museum, Shigaraki, Shiga, Japan,
1992–97. Öffentlich zugänglicher Museumsraum bietet
Aussicht auf die unberührte landschaftliche Umgebung.
Peis Glockenturm, der auch für die Glaubensgemeinschaft der Shûmeikai erbaut wurde, ist links in der Ferne
zu sehen.

I.M. Pei, Musée Miho, Shigaraki, Shiga, Japon,
1992–97. Les espaces publics du musée donnent sur
la campagne encore vierge. La tour-clocher de Pei,
également construite pour Shinji-Shûmeikai, s'aperçoit
dans le lointain, à gauche.

of the entrance doors framing a beautiful pine tree on the opposite side of the building is a touch recalling Chinese architecture
and painting, even as it reveals a truly Japanese landscape. No
other architect of our times could bring such cultural references
to bear on a museum project of this nature. More obviously
than in his many American buildings, in the Miho Museum
Pei combines his personal culture with that acquired in years of
experience in the United States. In his hands, deeply traditional
forms assume an undeniable modernity. Technically speaking,
few modern buildings have reached the standards of quality
of the Miho Museum, both because of the client's insistence on
the highest standards and because of Pei's vigilance, carried
through on the worksite by project architect Tim Culbert.

In a book entitled *The Unreal America, Architecture and Illusion*,
the doyenne of American architectural critics, Ada Louise
Huxtable, launched a scathing critique on contemporary American design, writing for example that "while high taste and low
taste have been consummating their union, a great divide has
opened between what is most serious and what is most popular
in the arts. In architecture, there is a growing chasm between
architects and their clients, between professionals and public, a
distancing of buildings and their users, a widening gap between
an increasingly complex and hermetic art and a product designed
for instant appeal and quick commercial success. Into this gap
has come escape architecture – the user-friendly substitutes,
the buildings-in-costume, and the pretend-places favored by
preservationists, builders, investors, and the consuming public.
Postmodernism has been a kind of revenge on modernism
among philistines and intellectuals alike, a comforting justification for a public that had stubbornly resisted both the modernist
aesthetic and morality."[9] In a catchphrase likely to be frequently
quoted, she concludes, "Today, form follows feeling... today
desire, not utility, dictates design." Ms. Huxtable makes specific
reference to the architecture of Disney, and lashes out with particular vigor against Peter Eisenman, writing, "...the self-absorption
of the present generation has contributed to a dismissal of social
needs in favor of arcane aesthetic exercises and narrow investiga-

nischen Ganzen. Titan, Kalkstein und Glas sind die wesentlichen Baumaterialien. Der größte Raum mißt 130 x 30 m und sieht aus wie das Innere eines vollkommen stützenfreien Schiffsrumpfes. Die meisten Ausstellungssäle sind etwa 6 m hoch und höher, so daß sie im Verbund mit dem phantastischen Atrium eine lichte Geräumigkeit erzeugen, die man sonst nur von Kathedralen kennt. Neben einer neuen, von Sir Norman Foster gestalteten U-Bahn-Linie und einer Brücke sowie dem Flughafengebäude von Santiago Calatrava verkündet das Guggenheim Museum den Glauben der Stadt Bilbao, der Region und der spanischen Zentralregierung an die Erneuerung dieses Industriestandorts durch zeitgenössische Architektur und modernes Design. So wie die großen Kathedralen vergangener Zeiten den Reichtum und die Macht ihrer Städte verkündeten, tun die Museen und anderen Kulturbauten dies heute in ähnlicher Weise. Es bleibt natürlich abzuwarten, ob diese Signale stark genug sind, um die öffentliche Meinung umzustimmen oder den ganzen »Betrieb« und das Leben einer Stadt zu verändern. Auf jeden Fall haben die Stadtbehörden von Bilbao bei diesem Projekt viel Geld investiert, und der Ertrag aus dieser Investition könnte tatsächlich zukünftige Stadtentwicklungen auf der ganzen Welt beeinflussen.

Ein Vergleich zwischen Meiers Getty Center und Gehrys Guggenheim Museum in Bilbao offenbart zwei sehr unterschiedliche Architekturtypen: ein fest in der mediterranen Tradition verwurzeltes Steingebäude und eine expressionistische, skulpturale Metallkonstruktion. Beide sind Ergebnisse einzigartiger Umstände, die sich in den kommenden Jahren höchstwahrscheinlich nicht bzw. nicht annähernd wiederholen werden. Wirtschaftliche Faktoren im besonderen und die Schöpferkraft der Gegenwartsarchitektur im allgemeinen werden wohl eher dazu führen, daß diese beiden Bauten künftig als kreative Höhepunkte der amerikanischen Architekten nach dem Zweiten Weltkrieg gelten werden. In Bezug auf das äußere Erscheinungsbild stellen sie fast diametrale Gegensätze dar und belegen das grundlegende Fehlen eines Zeitgeistes, der über das Gebot hinausdenkt, daß Kunst a priori höchstes Lob und äußerste An-

miques et la créativité de l'architecture contemporaine en général peuvent laisser penser que ces deux œuvres seront peut-être considérées comme le summum de l'inventivité des architectes américains de l'après-guerre. Quasi opposées sur le plan esthétique, elles prouvent le manque criant de zeitgeist en dehors du consensus sur le déploiement d'efforts que mérite l'activité artistique. Une époque qui s'attache autant à glorifier les activités artistiques n'est peut-être pas si mauvaise après tout.

À bien des égards, l'un des projets les plus exceptionnels et les plus étonnants présentés dans cet ouvrage est le Musée Miho d'I.M. Pei. Il a été érigé sur un spectaculaire terrain boisé dans une zone naturelle protégée des montagnes des environs de Shigaraki, préfecture de Shiga, à environ une heure et demie de voiture de Kyoto. On l'approche par un tunnel et un pont à haubans en post-tension, solutions choisies par l'architecte pour éviter dans la mesure du possible de porter atteinte au paysage. Une fois au pied des marches menant à l'entrée, le visiteur n'a guère idée de l'importance du volume des galeries, car 80% de leur surface se trouvent en sous-sol afin de respecter la stricte réglementation écologique locale. Le dessin de l'escalier qui conduit à la porte d'entrée et la silhouette du toit qui la surmonte évoquent un temple traditionnel japonais. Shinji-Shûmeikai, l'organisation qui a financé ce musée et le clocher achevée par Pei en 1990, se consacre à la recherche de la beauté dans la nature et l'art, et le musée illustre à de nombreux égards l'aboutissement de cette quête. Dans le remarquable soin porté aux détails et à la qualité de l'architecture comme dans la nature exceptionnelle des objets d'archéologie exposés, ce lieu est en soi une œuvre d'art d'exception. Pei se sert ici d'une pierre déjà utilisée sous la Pyramide du Louvre, et le dessin pyramidal des verrières rappelle également le musée parisien. Malgré ces similarités et les vicissitudes habituelles de la commande qui a connu des développements et des modifications structurelles même après le début du chantier, I. M. Pei, à 80 ans, confirme qu'il reste l'un des plus grands architectes contemporains. Dans la longue successions de ses grandes réalisations allant du Louvre à la Banque de Chine et à une œuvre en projet, le musée

tions of an intensely self-indulgent and almost incommunicable nature. One questions their value, beyond self-satisfaction. Only at this moment of retreat and introspection could a talent like Peter Eisenman's have flourished and had a following. He has created a theoretical, abstract architecture in which the building is its own meaning and reward, an autonomous and arbitrary geometry generated by rationalizations of equally abstract and arbitrary features of the site, or chaos theory, or whatever is in the latest vogue."

It is hard to deny many of the charges made by Ada Louise Huxtable against a part of contemporary American architecture, and yet, as the buildings published in this volume would tend to demonstrate, there is also a current of socially responsible, aesthetically creative work being done. At any time in recent history, the number of "quality" architects working, as opposed to those willing to erect whatever any corporate or private client desired, has been strictly limited. So too there are few painters or sculptures who can rightfully claim to be truly creative and something more than imitative. Robert Venturi long ago pointed out the underlying interest of architecture in places like Las Vegas in his two books, *Complexity and Contradiction in Architecture,* and *Learning from Las Vegas.* It doesn't take much perspicacity to notice that contemporary architecture in the United States (like that of Japan, England or Argentina) is usually rather bad and uninventive. The interesting work, the creative work, is always being built at the margin, by figures such as Sambo Mockbee and the Rural Studio at one end of the scale, and I.M. Pei at the other. It can only be hoped that their example will inspire others.

1 "Howard's House," *Architecture,* July 1997.
2 Goldberger, Paul: "Michael Rotondi, a Contemporary Villa Embraces the New Jersey Landscape," *Architectural Digest,* March 1997.
3 Moonan, Wendy: "A Mathematical Ordering System Helped Roto Architects Sculpt a Complex Scheme," *Architectural Record,* April 1997.
4 LeBlanc, Sydney: "From Humble Sources, Earthy Elegance Springs," *The New York Times,* April 18, 1996.
5 *Steven Holl.* GA Document Extra 06, ADA Edita, Tokyo, 1996.
6 Holl, Steven: *Intertwining.* Princeton Architectural Press, New York, 1996.
7 Giovanni, Joseph: "Modern Reliquary," *Architecture,* April 1997.
8 Jencks, Charles: "Gehry in Bilbao," *Interiors,* August 1997.
9 Huxtable, Ada Louise: *"The Unreal America, Architecture and Illusion."* The New Press, New York, 1997.

strengungen verdient. Eine Zeit, welche die Kunst verherrlicht, ist vielleicht nicht so schlecht, wie manche offenbar glauben.

In mehr als einer Hinsicht ist das ungewöhnlichste in diesem Buch vorgestellte Gebäude I.M. Peis Miho Museum in den Bergen bei Shigaraki in der japanischen Präfektur Shiga. Da das herrliche Waldgrundstück sich in einem Naturschutzgebiet befindet, entschied sich der Architekt für Zufahrt und Zugang zum Museum durch einen Tunnel und über eine Spanndraht-brücke, um die Naturlandschaft so wenig wie möglich zu beeinträchtigen. Wenn der Besucher auf den Stufen vor dem Eingang steht, kann er kaum ahnen, wie groß die Ausstellungsräume wirklich sind, denn das Museum ist in Erfüllung der strengen Umweltgesetze Japans zu über 80% in den Erdboden eingelassen. Schon die Stufen, die zur Eingangstür führen, und die von dort sichtbaren Dachumrisse vermitteln allerdings deutlich, daß den Besucher innen ein ähnliches Raumerlebnis erwartet wie in einem japanischen Tempel. Shinji-Shûmeikai, Bauherr des Miho Museums und eines Glockenturms, den Pei 1990 fertigstellte, ist eine Glaubensgemeinschaft, die sich der Schönheit von Natur und Kunst verschrieben hat, und das Museumsgebäude stellt auf vielfältige Weise die Erfüllung dieser Bemühungen dar. Sowohl die Qualität der Details und der gesamten architektonischen Gestaltung als auch die Ausgrabungsstücke machen das Museum zu einem einzigartigen Gesamtkunstwerk. Pei hat den gleichen Stein verwendet, den er schon im Unterbau der Louvre-Glaspyramide einsetzte, und auch die pyramidenförmigen Deckenoberlichter erinnern an das Pariser Museum. Trotz dieser Ähnlichkeiten und der ungewöhnlichen Gegebenheiten der Bauaufgabe, die noch während der Bauzeit zu Erweiterungen und Überarbeitungen der Konstruktion führten, bestätigt I.M. Pei in seinem achtzigsten Lebensjahr, daß er in vielerlei Hinsicht der bedeutendste aller lebenden Architekten ist. Im Kontext seiner zahlreichen in den letzten Jahren erstellten Großbauten hebt sich das Miho Museum als besonderes Juwel von den anderen ab, weil es gegen alle Wahrscheinlichkeit in einer völlig abgeschiedenen Gegend in Japan gebaut wurde. Es ist zwar tief im Boden und in den Traditionen Japans verwurzelt, doch hat Pei

Sambo Mockbee and the Rural Studio, Harris House,
Mason's Bend, Alabama, 1995–97. A "butterfly roof"
facilitates natural ventilation.

Sambo Mockbee mit Rural Studio, Harris House,
Mason's Bend, Alabama, 1995–97. Ein
»Schmetterlingsdach« ermöglicht natürliche
Belüftung.

Sambo Mockbee et le Rural Studio, Harris House,
Mason's Bend, Alabama, 1995–97. Le toit «en ailes
de papillon» facilite la ventilation naturelle.

de Miho se détache tel un joyau, isolé au cœur de l'une des régions les plus reculées du Japon. Bien qu'il soit profondément enraciné dans le sol et la tradition de ce pays, il n'en a pas moins été dessiné par un architecte qui n'a pas oublié sa Chine natale. Il a ainsi fait ressortir la similarité du site avec certains paysages chinois, et c'est une connaissance partagée des auteurs classiques de son pays d'origine qui lui a permis de nouer une relation très proche avec l'ancienne responsable de Shinji-Shûmeikai, Mohoko Koyama, relation poursuivie avec sa fille, Hiroko Koyama. L'ouverture circulaire des portes d'entrée, encadrant un superbe pin planté de l'autre côté du bâtiment, rappelle l'architecture et la peinture chinoises, même si elle révèle un paysage authentiquement nippon. Aucun autre architecte contemporain ne pouvait faire naître de telles références à partir d'un projet muséal de cette nature. De façon encore plus évidente que dans ses nombreuses réalisations américaines, Pei combine dans ce musée Miho sa culture personnelle avec l'expérience acquise au cours de ses longues années passées aux États-Unis. Entre ses mains, des formes authentiquement traditionnelles prennent une modernité indéniable. Sur un plan technique, peu de réalisations modernes ont atteint des standards de qualité aussi élevés que le musée Miho, à la fois par la volonté de perfection du client et par la vigilance de Pei, relayé sur le chantier par l'architecte de projet Tim Culbert.

Dans un livre intitulé «The Unreal America, Architecture and Illusion» (L'Amérique irréelle, architecture et illusion), la doyenne des critiques d'architecture américains, Ada Louise Huxtable, a lancé une cinglante attaque contre la création contemporaine en Amérique, écrivant, par exemple, qu'«alors que le grand goût et le goût populaire consomment leur union, une énorme faille s'est ouverte dans les arts entre le plus sérieux et le plus populaire. En architecture se constate un chiasme grandissant entre les architectes et leurs clients, entre les professionnels et le public, une distanciation de plus en plus forte entre les bâtiments et leurs usagers, une séparation de plus en plus grande entre un art de plus en plus hermétique et complexe et un produit conçu pour une séduction immédiate et un succès

beim Entwurf auch sein Heimatland China vor Augen gehabt. Er unterstreicht die Ähnlichkeit des Standorts mit chinesischen Landschaften. Die runde Öffnung der Eingangstüren rahmt das Bild einer Kiefer ein, die auf der anderen Seite des Gebäudes steht. Dies wirkt wie chinesische Architektur und Malerei, obwohl hier eine echt japanische Landschaft dargestellt wird. Viel offensichtlicher als in seinen vielen Bauten in Amerika kombiniert Pei im Miho Museum die Kultur seiner eigenen Heimat China mit seinen über Jahrzehnte in den USA erworbenen Erfahrungen. Unter seinen Händen werden althergebrachte Formen unleugbar modern.

In dem Buch »The Unreal America, Architecture and Illusion« verfaßte die einflußreiche Architekturkritikerin Ada Louise Huxtable eine schneidende Kritik an der amerikanischen Gegenwartsarchitektur: »... während guter und schlechter Geschmack die Ehe vollzogen haben, hat sich zwischen dem Ernsthaftesten und dem Beliebtesten in der Kunst ein breiter Abgrund aufgetan. In der Architektur weitet sich die Kluft zwischen Architekten und ihren Bauherren, zwischen Fachleuten und Öffentlichkeit. Gebäude entfernen sich von ihren Nutzern, und der Graben zwischen einer zunehmend komplexen, sich abschottenden Kunst und dem für sofortigen Verbrauch und schnellen kommerziellen Erfolg entworfenen Produkt wird immer unüberbrückbarer. Hier setzt die Flucht-Architektur ein, mit nutzerfreundlichen Substituten, Gebäuden in Maske und Kostüm und Kunstwelten, die bei Denkmal- und Umweltschützern, Bauunternehmern, Investoren und Konsumenten gleichermaßen beliebt sind. Die Postmoderne ist für Spießer wie für Intellektuelle zu einer Art Racheakt gegen die Moderne geworden, tröstliche Rechtfertigung der breiten Masse, die sich sowohl der modernen Ästhetik wie auch der neuen Moral hartnäckig widersetzte.«[9] Ihre Schlußfolgerung (die wahrscheinlich zum vielzitierten Schlagwort avancieren wird) heißt: »Heute folgt die Form dem Gefühl ... heute wird die Gestaltung vom Wunsch diktiert, nicht vom Nutzen.« Frau Huxtable bezieht sich auf die Disney-Architektur und wütet gegen Peter Eisenman, wenn sie schreibt: »... die heutige Generation konzentriert sich nur auf das eigene

commercial rapide. Dans cette faille s'est infiltrée une architecture d'évasion (ces substituts conviviaux, bâtiments travestis, faux-semblants appréciés des conservateurs, des promoteurs, des investisseurs et des consommateurs). Le postmodernisme avait fourni une sorte de revanche sur le modernisme aux philistins comme aux intellectuels, et une justification réconfortante pour un public qui avait résisté avec obstination à l'esthétique et à la morale modernistes.»[9] Dans une formule qui sera sans doute souvent citée, elle conclut: «Aujourd'hui, la forme suit le sentiment... aujourd'hui, c'est le désir et non l'utilité qui dicte la création.» A.L. Huxtable fait une référence spécifique à l'architecture Disney, et se déchaîne avec une vigueur particulière contre Peter Eisenman, écrivant: «... l'auto-complaisance de la génération actuelle a contribué à renoncer à prendre en compte les besoins sociaux en faveur d'exercices esthétiques obscurs et de recherches étroites d'une nature personnelle et presque incommunicable. On peut questionner leur valeur, au-delà de l'autosatisfaction. Ce n'est que dans une telle période de reflux et d'introspection qu'un talent comme celui de Peter Eisenman a pu se développer et se faire connaître. Il a créé une architecture théorique abstraite dans laquelle le bâti est sa propre signification et sa propre récompense, une géométrie autonome et arbitraire générée par des rationalisations de caractéristiques tout aussi abstraites et arbitraires du site, ou de la théorie du chaos, ou de tout ce qui est à la dernière mode.»

Il est difficile de réfuter nombreuses charges d'Ada Louise Huxtable contre une partie de l'architecture américaine, et cependant, comme les réalisations publiées dans ce volume tendent à le prouver, il existe néanmoins un courant d'œuvres esthétiquement créatives et socialement responsables. À toute époque de l'histoire récente, le nombre d'architectes de «qualité», par rapport à ceux prêts à répondre au moindre désir de leurs clients commerciaux ou privés, a toujours été strictement limité. De même, peu de peintures ou de sculptures peuvent prétendre à juste titre d'être authentiquement créatives et un peu plus qu'une simple imitation. Robert Venturi faisait remarquer, il y a longtemps, l'intérêt sous-jacent de l'architecture de lieux

Ich, was dazu beigetragen hat, daß soziale Bedürfnisse hintangesetzt werden zugunsten von geheimnisvollen ästhetischen Übungen und Untersuchungen einer hemmungslos selbstbezogenen und fast nicht vermittelbaren Art. Man muß ihren Wert – außer zur Selbstbefriedigung – in Frage stellen. Nur in dieser Zeit des allgemeinen Rückzugs auf sich selbst konnte ein Talent wie Peter Eisenman überhaupt hochkommen und Einfluß gewinnen. Er hat eine theoretische, abstrakte Architektur geschaffen, in der das Bauwerk sich selbst Sinn und Lohn genug ist, eine autonome, willkürliche Geometrie, die er ebenso abstrakt und willkürlich aus dem Baugelände oder der Chaostheorie – oder was sonst gerade der letzte Schrei ist – ableitet.«

Viele der von Ada Louise Huxtable geäußerten Vorwürfe sind nur schwer zu entkräften. Dennoch zeigen die in diesem Band vorgestellten Bauten, daß viele Architekten sozial verantwortliche und ästhetisch schöpferische Arbeit leisten. Die Anzahl der Architekten, die »beste Qualität« liefern, ist in den vergangenen Jahren eng begrenzt gewesen – im Gegensatz zur Zahl derer, die bereitwillig errichtet haben, was immer ihre Auftraggeber haben wollten. Ebenso gibt es nur wenige Maler oder Bildhauer, die mit Recht von sich sagen können, sie seien wirklich kreativ und mehr als nur Imitatoren. In seinen beiden Büchern »Complexity and Contradiction in Architecture« und »Learning from Las Vegas« hat Robert Venturi vor vielen Jahren auf den Nutzen der Architektur an Orten wie Las Vegas hingewiesen. Man braucht keinen großen Scharfblick, um zu erkennen, daß die Gegenwartsarchitektur in den Vereinigten Staaten – genau wie in Japan, Großbritannien oder Argentinien – im Schnitt ziemlich schlecht und einfallslos ist. Die interessanten, originellen Werke sind immer »Randerscheinungen« und werden von Leuten wie Sambo Mockbee und seinem Rural Studio am einen oder I.M. Pei am anderen Ende der Skala geschaffen. Man kann nur hoffen, daß ihr Beispiel Schule machen wird.

comme Las Vegas dans deux ouvrages, «Complexité et Contradiction en Architecture» et «L'Enseignement de Las Vegas». Il ne faut pas une perspicacité exceptionnelle pour noter que l'architecture contemporaine américaine (comme celle du Japon, de la Grande-Bretagne ou de l'Argentine) est généralement assez piètre et sans grande invention. L'œuvre intéressante, l'œuvre créative est toujours marginale, qu'elle soit signée par des personnalités comme Sambo Mockbee et le Rural Studio d'un côté ou I.M. Pei de l'autre. On ne peut qu'espérer que leur exemple deviendra une source d'inspiration.

Gail Vittori & Pliny Fisk III

Center for Maximum Potential Building Systems

Pliny Fisk III has been the Co-Director of the Center for Maximum Potential Building Systems, a non-profit organization based in Austin, Texas, since 1975 with his partner Gail Vittori. Although Pliny Fisk is the principal designer of the Advanced Green Builder Demonstration published here, neither he nor Gail Vittori are licensed architects. The fact that their project was the only one in the United States recognized by the 1992 Rio Summit conference on the environment is an indication that their approach is somewhat outside of the mainstream of American architecture. And yet ecological concerns are naturally very present in the work of numerous recognized designers in the United States. It can be said that the approach of Fisk and Vittori is radical in that they appear to have sought out every conceivable way to make their house and workplace environmentally responsible, right down to conceiving of its eventual dismantlement so that the construction materials will not be wasted. The aesthetics of the Advanced Green Builder Demonstration are indeed mainly the product of its specific goals and functions. It is not beautiful in the traditional sense of the word, but Fisk and Vittori seem to be pleading for a new definition of such terms as they are applied to architecture.

Pliny Fisk III. leitet zusammen mit seiner Partnerin Gail Vittori seit 1975 das Center for Maximum Potential Building Systems in Austin, Texas, eine gemeinnützige Institution zur Entwicklung optimaler Bausysteme. Obwohl Fisk der erste Entwurfsarchitekt der hier vorgestellten »Advanced Green Builder Demonstration« war, besitzen weder er noch Vittori die Zulassung zum Architekten. Die Tatsache, daß ihr Projekt als einziges aus den USA beim Umweltgipfel in Rio 1992 präsentiert wurde, weist ihre Arbeit sozusagen als Randerscheinung der amerikanischen Architektur aus. Dennoch sind ökologische Überlegungen natürlich im Schaffen vieler anerkannter Architekten in den Vereinigten Staaten präsent. Man kann sagen, daß Fisks und Vittoris Gestaltungsweise radikal ist, und zwar weil sie offenbar jede nur erdenkliche Chance genutzt haben, ein »umweltverantwortliches« Haus zu bauen – bis hin zur bereits eingeplanten späteren Demontage, damit die Baustoffe nicht verschwendet werden. Das Erscheinungsbild des Musterhauses ist tatsächlich vor allem das Ergebnis seiner spezifischen Ziele und Funktionen. Es ist nicht schön im herkömmlichen Sinne des Wortes. Fisk und Vittori scheinen für eine neue Definition von Schönheit – auf Architektur angewandt – zu plädieren.

Pliny Fisk III co-dirige avec Gail Vittori le Center for Maximum Potential Building Systems, organisme à but non lucratif basé à Austin, Texas, depuis 1975. Bien qu'il soit le principal concepteur de l'«Advanced Green Builder Demonstration», publié ici, ni lui ni Gail Vittori ne possèdent de licence professionnelle d'architecte. Le fait que leur projet ait été la seule réalisation américaine reconnue par la Conférence du Sommet de la Terre – Rio de Janeiro 1992 – montre que leur approche reste en marge du courant principal de l'architecture américaine, même si les préoccupations écologiques sont très présentes par nature dans l'œuvre de nombreux praticiens aux États-Unis. L'approche de Fisk et Vittori est radicale dans la mesure où ils semblent avoir exploré toutes les voies possibles pour rendre écologique cette maison-lieu de travail, de sa conception à sa démolition, afin d'éviter le gaspillage des matériaux de construction. L'esthétique de l'Advanced Green Builder Demonstration est essentiellement le produit de ses objectifs et de ses fonctions. La maison n'est certes pas superbe, au sens traditionnel du mot, mais Fisk et Vittori plaident pour une nouvelle définition des qualificatifs subjectifs en architecture.

CMPBS, Advanced Green Builder Demonstration, Austin, Texas, 1994–97.

Advanced Green Builder Demonstration

Austin, Texas, 1994–1997

The goal of Pliny Fisk and Gail Vittori was to create a home and workplace that would maximize sensitivity to environmental issues. Clearly, the functional aspects of this 170 square meter building in the broad sense of the word took priority over any purely aesthetic considerations. Highly visible cisterns designed to contain more than 50,000 liters of rainwater are just one example of this aspect of the building. Local materials that do not damage the environment were chosen, such as straw from the Texas grasslands to make the clay walls and plywood panels. Flexibility of the installations is another priority of this husband and wife team, as is a willingness to make do with 100 liters of water a day for a family of four (average U.S. consumption is four times higher), or with a very small bathroom to further avoid waste, for example. Waste is even avoided in the potential for easy disassembly, which is part of the design. The announced cost of the building is $150,000, while approximately $100,000 was spent on preliminary research and prototype development.

Pliny Fisk und Gail Vittori wollten ein Wohnhaus mit Arbeitsplatz schaffen, das in optimaler Weise Rücksichtnahme auf ökologische Belange demonstriert. Die funktionellen Aspekte dieses 170 m² umfassenden Hauses hatten im weitesten Sinne Vorrang vor rein ästhetischen Überlegungen. Höchst auffällige Zisternen mit einem Fassungsvermögen von über 50000 Liter Regenwasser sind hierfür nur ein Beispiel. Das Architekten-Ehepaar wählte örtlich vorhandene Baustoffe, die die Umwelt nicht schädigen, unter anderem Stroh für die Lehmwände und als Füllung für die Sperrholztafeln. Ganz besonders wichtig ist für Fisk und Vittori die Flexibilität der Installation sowie die Bereitschaft, mit 100 Litern Wasser pro Tag auszukommen – und das für eine vierköpfige Familie (der Durchschnittsverbrauch ist in den USA viermal so hoch). Ebenso ist das Haus lediglich mit einem sehr kleinen Badezimmer ausgestattet, um Verschwendung zu vermeiden. Geringere Abfallmengen sind im Entwurf bereits dadurch eingeplant, daß eine leichte Demontage des ganzen Hauses möglich sein wird. Die Baukosten wurden mit 150000 $ angegeben, wobei etwa 100000 $ für Vorstudien und Prototypenentwicklung ausgegeben wurden.

L'objectif de Pliny Fisk et de Gail Vittori était de créer une maison-lieu-de-travail qui traduise une sensibilité maximum aux enjeux écologiques. Les aspects fonctionnels de cette construction de 170 m² ont à l'évidence bénéficié d'une priorité sur les considérations purement esthétiques. Des citernes très visibles, conçues pour contenir plus de 50000 l d'eau de pluie, illustrent cette démarche. Des matériaux locaux et écologiques ont été choisis, comme la paille du Texas pour les murs d'argile et des panneaux de contreplaqué. La souplesse des installations constitue une autre priorité de ce couple d'architectes, de même que sa volonté d'apporter un confort suffisant malgré une consommation d'eau quotidienne de 100 l pour une famille de quatre personnes, soit quatre fois moins que la consommation américaine moyenne, ou une salle de bain très petite pour limiter le gaspillage. Celui-ci est pris en compte jusque dans la démolition-recyclage de la maison conçu dès le départ. Le coût annoncé du bâtiment s'élève à 900000 F, et 600000 F environ ont été dépensé pour les études préliminaires et la mise au point du prototype.

Page 49: The drawing, including an elevation and floor plan, shows the round volumes of the cisterns designed to contain more than 50,000 liters of rain water.

Seite 49: In den Zeichnungen – u.a. Aufriß und Grundriß – sind auch die runden Zisternen zu sehen, die über 50000 Liter Regenwasser speichern können.

Page 49: Le dessin, l'élévation et le plan au sol montrent les volumes cylindriques des citernes conçues pour contenir plus de 50000 l d'eau de pluie.

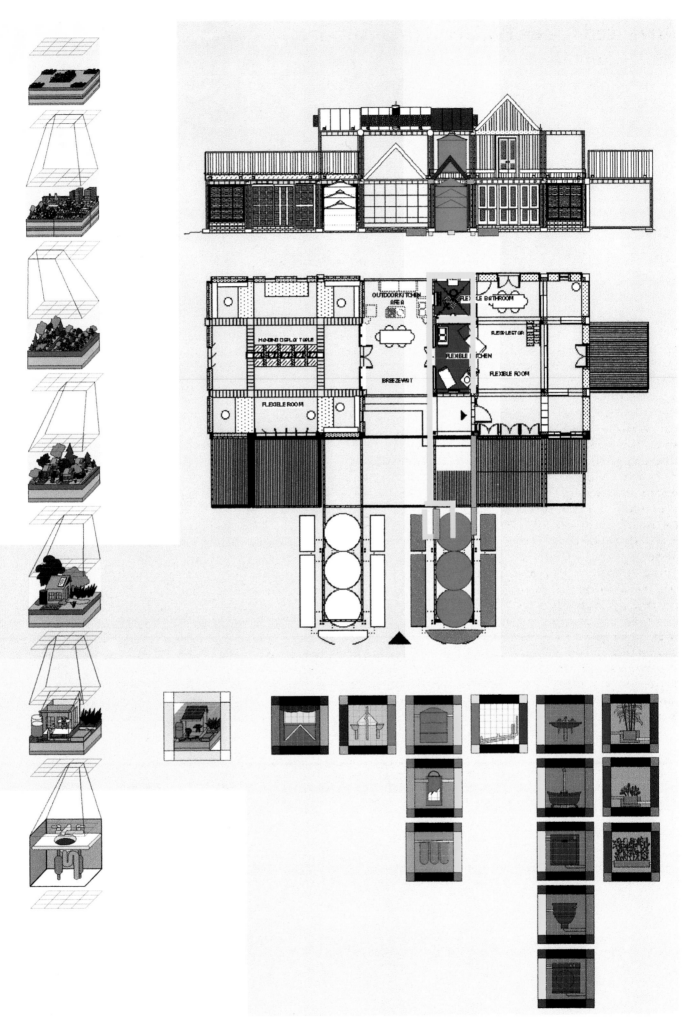

A modular steel skeleton permits the house to be easily put together and disassembled in various different forms. Ornamental reeds and food producing vines are used to shade the building.

Ein Stahlskelett aus Moduleinheiten erleichtert die Montage des Hauses in verschiedenen Konfigurationen und ebenso die mühelose Demontage. Schilfrohr und Kletterwein wurden angepflanzt und bieten Sonnenschutz.

L'ossature modulaire en acier permet de monter ou de remonter aisément la maison sous des formes différentes. Des joncs d'ornement et des vignes protègent le bâtiment du soleil.

Although the brame of this building is welded together, a future version will have special fasteners to make the structure even easier to disassemble. The spaces are intended to be as open and flexible as possible.

Das Stahlskelett dieses Hauses ist zwar verschweißt, bei künftigen Ausführungen wird man aber spezielle Befestigungsteile einsetzen, damit das Gebäude noch leichter zu demontieren ist. Die Innenräume sollten so offen und flexibel wie möglich sein.

Bien que l'ossature soit soudée, une version ultérieure devrait bénéficier d'un système spécial de fixations qui en facilitera le démontage. Les espaces sont conçus pour être aussi ouverts et polyvalents que possible.

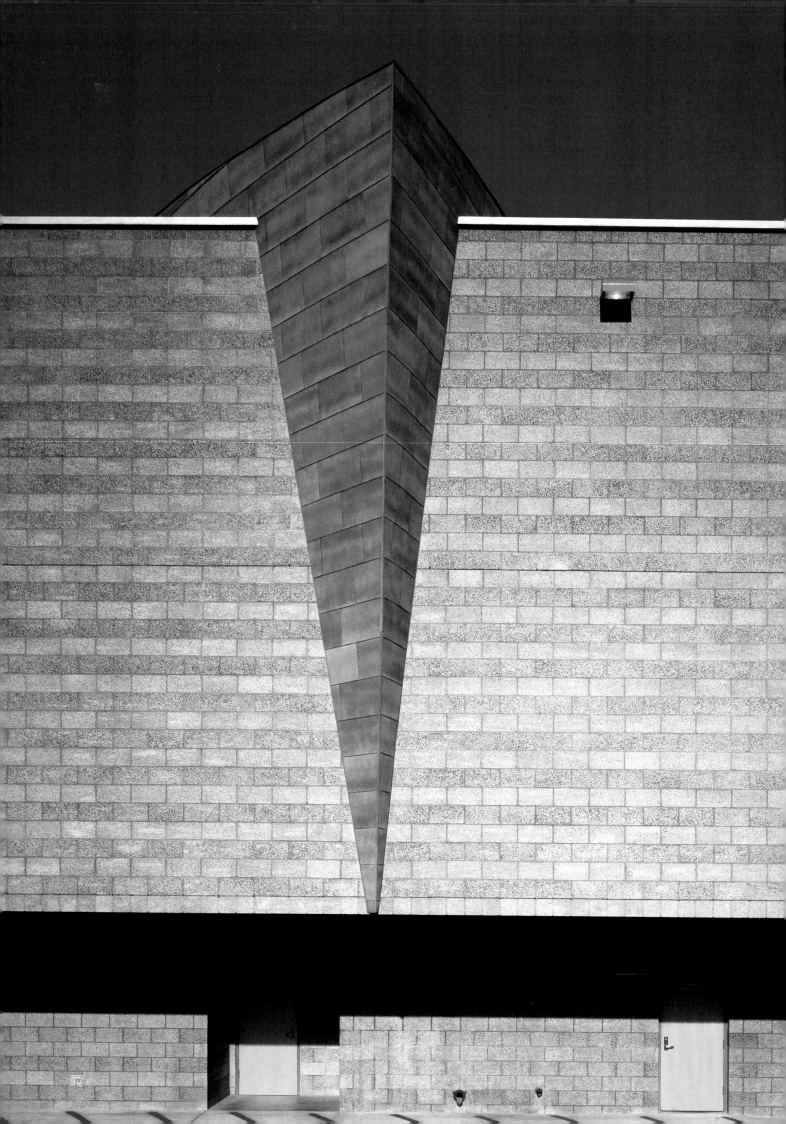

Steven Ehrlich

Born in 1946, Steven Ehrlich has used experience working in North and West Africa and Japan to create a personal style intended to blend Los Angeles tradition and architectural innovation. His homes have often included courtyards that bring nature into his architecture, creating an environment that he sees as a "cleansing from the outside world." In the 1990s he has branched out into larger projects, with the 1991 Shatto Recreation Center (Los Angeles, California, 1991), which *Newsweek* called a "graceful example of defensive architecture," the Sony Music Entertainment Campus (Santa Monica, California, 1993), a 9,500 square meter complex blending indoor and outdoor space, and more recently, the 32,000 square meter Dreamworth S.K.G. Animation Studios in Glendale, California.

Steven Ehrlich wurde 1946 in New York geboren. Aus beruflichen Erfahrungen in Nord- und Westafrika sowie in Japan formte sich ein persönlicher Stil, dessen erklärtes Ziel es ist, die Traditionen von Los Angeles mit architektonischen Innovationen zu verbinden. Seine Wohnungen besitzen beispielsweise häufig Innenhöfe, so daß die Natur in seine Architektur einbezogen und eine Umgebung geschaffen wird, die er als »Ort der spirituellen Reinigung von der Außenwelt« sieht. In den 90er Jahren hat Ehrlich sich zunehmend mit größeren Projekten befaßt, etwa dem Shatto Recreation Center (Los Angeles, Kalifornien, 1991) das die Zeitschrift »Newsweek« als »anmutiges Beispiel defensiver Architektur« bezeichnete, dem Sony Music Entertainment Campus (Santa Monica, Kalifornien, 1993), einem 9500 m² umfassenden Komplex mit ineinander übergehenden Innen- und Außenräumen, oder in jüngster Zeit die Dreamworth S.K.G. Animation Studios in Glendale, Kalifornien, mit 32 000 m².

Né en 1946, Steven Ehrlich a mis à profit son expérience acquise en Afrique du Nord et de l'Ouest ainsi qu'au Japon pour se créer un style personnel qui associe l'innovation architecturale et la tradition de Los Angeles. Ses maisons possèdent souvent des cours fermées qui laissent entrer la nature dans l'architecture, et créent un environnement qu'il voit comme une «épuration du monde extérieur». Dans les années 90, il s'est lancé dans des projets plus importants, comme le Shatto Recreation Center (Los Angeles, Californie, 1991) que «Newsweek» a qualifié de «gracieux exemple d'architecture défensive», et le Sony Music Entertainment Campus (Santa Monica, Californie, 1993), complexe de 9 500 m² associant espaces intérieurs et extérieurs, ou, plus récemment encore, les Dreamworth S.K.G. Animation Studios à Glendale, Californie (32 000 m²).

Steven Ehrlich, Robertson Branch Library, Los Angeles, California, 1993–97.

Steven Ehrlich, Robertson Branch Library, Los Angeles, Kalifornien, 1993–97.

Steven Ehrlich, Robertson Branch Library, Los Angeles, Californie, 1993–97.

Robertson Branch Library
Los Angeles, California, 1993–1997

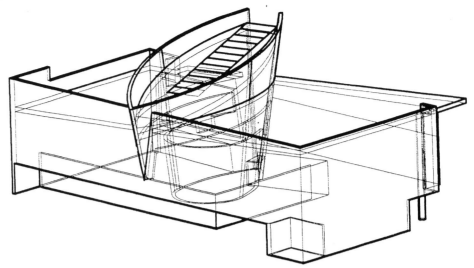

Located on Robertson Boulevard about a ten minute drive from Culver City, this building was designed to "announce the importance of the library both to the community and to the casual passerby." A copper-clad element shaped like "the hull of a boat" slices through the rectangular volume, which measures roughly 1,000 square meters in floor area. In collaboration with the artist Erika Rothernberg, Steven Ehrlich used this element like a "marquee" or billboard to highlight a certain number of "witticisms or pithy literary quotations." A testimony both to the importance of the car in Los Angeles, and to the restricted size of the site, about three quarters of the ground level space is used for parking. The remaining quarter on the first floor is devoted to a community room and offices, while the reading area and books are located on the second floor. Though in a sense typical of Los Angeles, the Robertson Branch Library also demonstrates the willingness of talented contemporary architects to take on projects that are modest in both size and budget.

Der Bibliotheks-Neubau steht am Robertson Boulevard, zehn Autominuten von Culver City entfernt. Er sollte sowohl die Ortsgemeinde als auch Passanten auf die Bedeutung der Bibliothek hinweisen. Ein kupferverkleideter »Schiffsrumpf« durchstößt den rechteckigen, kastenförmigen Baukörper, der etwa 1000 m² Nutzfläche bietet. In Zusammenarbeit mit der Künstlerin Erika Rothernberg hat Ehrlich dieses Element wie ein Sonnenvordach genutzt oder als Anschlagtafel für »eine Reihe geistreicher Bonmots und prägnanter Literaturzitate«. Die Tatsache, daß dreiviertel der nicht sehr großen Grundstücksfläche mit Parkplätzen belegt ist, weist auf die Bedeutung des Autos für Los Angeles hin. Im verbleibenden Viertel befinden sich ein Saal und Büros, während Leseraum und Büchersäle im 1. Obergeschoß untergebracht sind. Obschon in gewisser Weise typisch für Los Angeles, belegt die Robertson Branch Library die Bereitschaft begabter Architekten, auch kleinere Projekte mit niedrigerem Budget zu übernehmen.

En bordure de Robertson Boulevard, à dix minutes en voiture de Culver City, ce bâtiment veut «proclamer l'importance de la bibliothèque auprès des habitants du quartier et des passants». Un élément plaqué de cuivre en forme de «quille de navire» vient trancher le parallélépipède rectangulaire de 1000 m² de surface au sol environ. En collaboration avec l'artiste Erika Rothernberg, Steven Ehrlich a utilisé cet élément comme une marquise ou un panneau d'affichage pour mettre en scène des «jeux de mots ou citations littéraires lapidaires». Illustration du rôle de la voiture et des dimensions réduites du terrain, les trois quarts environ de la surface du rez-de-chaussée servent au stationnement. Le quart restant est consacré à une salle de réunion et à des bureaux, tandis que les zones de lecture et les livres sont en étage. Bien que typiquement de Los Angeles en un sens, la Robertson Branch Library démontre également que des architectes contemporains de talent ne refusent pas les projets de taille et de budget modestes.

A drawing and an interior view show how the irregular volume is inserted into the rectangular mass of the building.

Eine Zeichnung und eine Innenansicht zeigen, wie der unregelmäßige Baukörper in die rechteckige Gebäudeform eingefügt ist.

Dessin et vue intérieure montrant la manière dont le volume irrégulier s'insère dans la masse rectangulaire du bâtiment.

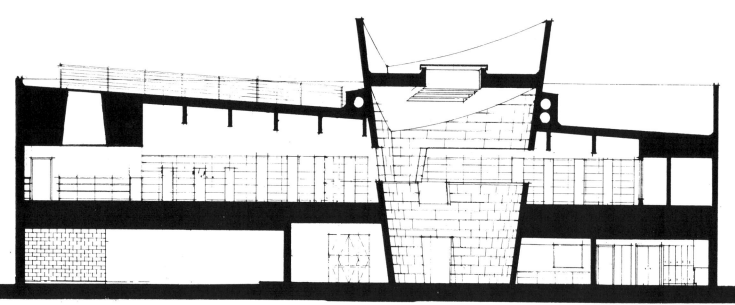

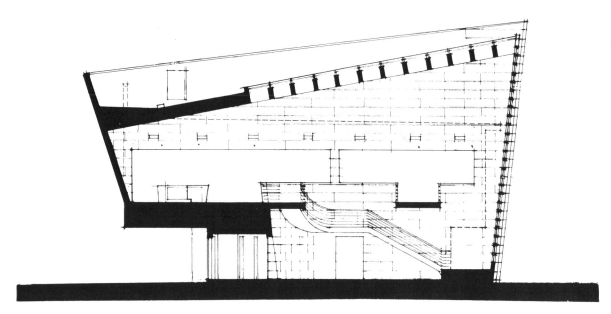

Side and frontal elevations show how the central volume cuts through the building, and how it is elevated to make way for parking space. To the right, the central stairway.

Zwei Aufrisse zeigen, wie der mittlere Baukörper das Gebäude durchschneidet. Es ist zudem erhöht, so daß darunter Platz für parkende Autos ist. Rechts das Haupttreppenhaus.

Élévations frontale et latérale montrant la pénétration du volume central dans le bâtiment, et sa surélévation pour laisser place au parking. À droite, l'escalier central.

Frank O. Gehry

Born in Toronto, Canada, in 1929, Frank O. Gehry is one of the most influential architects working today. Not only has he successfully called into question the forms that modern architecture has taken for granted, daring to use purely sculptural volumes, but he has done the same for materials of construction. It is not that steel and concrete are absent from his work, but rather that chain link, corrugated aluminum, or titanium cladding are present. Gehry seems to be as much at ease building a giant fish (Fishdance Restaurant, Kobe, Japan, 1984) as he is with an office building whose facade is dominated by a huge pair of binoculars (designed by Claes Oldenburg for Chiat/Day, Venice, California, 1989). His recent American Center in Paris met with criticism over design, and closed for budgetary reasons shortly after its completion. The Guggenheim Museum Bilbao published here has been hailed as one of his most significant works, while his first very large building in California, the Walt Disney Concert Hall in Los Angeles, will finally be built in 2001.

Frank O. Gehry wurde 1929 in Toronto, Kanada, geboren und gehört zu den einflußreichsten Architekten unserer Zeit. Er hat mit Erfolg Formen und Baumethoden hinterfragt, die für die moderne Architektur selbstverständlich waren, und es gewagt, rein plastisch geformte Baukörper zu schaffen. In seinem Werk sind Stahl und Beton durchaus vorhanden, er verwendet aber auch Kettenglieder, Aluminiumwellblech und Verkleidungen aus Titan. Gehry entwirft offenbar einen riesigen Fisch (Fishdance Restaurant, Kobe, Japan, 1984) ebenso mühelos wie ein Bürogebäude, dessen Fassade von einem gewaltigen Fernglas beherrscht wird (Claes Oldenburgs Entwurf für Chiat/Day, Venice, Kalifornien, 1989). Sein neues American Center in Paris stieß in bezug auf seine Gestaltung auf Kritik und mußte kurz nach der Eröffnung aus finanziellen Gründen wieder schließen. Das hier vorgestellte Guggenheim Museum in Bilbao gilt allgemein als eines seiner bedeutendsten Werke. Gehrys Walt Disney Concert Hall in Los Angeles soll nun nach langen Verzögerungen bis zum Jahr 2001 vollendet sein.

Frank O. Gehry, né en 1929 à Toronto, est l'un des plus influents architectes contemporains. Non seulement il a su remettre en question avec succès des formes que l'architecture moderne tenait pour établies et oser mettre en œuvre des volumes de sculpture pure, mais il a agi de même avec les matériaux de construction. Si l'acier et le béton sont présents dans ses réalisations, il aime également le treillage métallique, la tôle ondulée en aluminium ou les planches de bois brut. Gehry semble être aussi à l'aise dans la construction d'un poisson géant (Fishdance Restaurant, Kobe, Japon, 1984) que dans celle d'un immeuble de bureaux dont la façade est dominée par une énorme paire de jumelles (dessinée par Claes Oldenburg pour Chiat/Day, Venice, Californie, 1989). Son récent American Center à Paris a été critiqué pour sa conception, et fermé pour raisons budgétaires peu après son achèvement. Le Musée Guggenheim de Bilbao a été salué comme l'une de ses œuvres les plus significatives, alors qu'il semble que son premier grand chantier californien, celui du Walt Disney Concert Hall à Los Angeles, sera terminé en 2001.

Page 60: Frank O. Gehry, Guggenheim Museum Bilbao, Bilbao, Spain, 1991–97.
Pages 62–63: A view of the museum from across the Nervión River.

Seite 60: Frank O. Gehry, Guggenheim Museum Bilbao, Bilbao, Spanien, 1991–97.
Seite 62–63: Blick auf das Museum vom gegenüberliegenden Ufer des Flusses Nervión.

Page 60: Frank O. Gehry, Musée Guggenheim de Bilbao, Bilbao, Espagne, 1991–97.
Pages 62–63: Vue du musée prise de l'autre rive du Nervión.

Guggenheim Museum Bilbao

Bilbao, Spain, 1991–1997

The Guggenheim Museum Bilbao is without any doubt one of Frank O. Gehry's most spectacular architectural works. Here, the complex forms he has been studying and proposing for a number of years, for projects like the as yet unbuilt Walt Disney Concert Hall in Los Angeles, come together in a symphony of sculptural volumes. Part of a $1.5 billion redevelopment for this industrial city of the semi-autonomous Basque region, which includes a subway line designed by Sir Norman Foster, and a footbridge and airport by Santiago Calatrava, the new structure has a total floor area of 24,000 square meters with 10,600 square meters of exhibition area on three levels. Financed by the city, region, and Spanish government, the contents of the museum are in good part the responsibility of the Guggenheim Museum in New York, which has made several attempts to expand towards Europe under its dynamic director Thomas Krens. The new museum is an eminently urban structure, located on the banks of the Nervión River and literally crossed through by the Puente de la Salve bridge, which runs above part of the main exhibition gallery.
From the outside, its most spectacular feature is the titanium cladding of its "metallic flower" shapes, which were modeled by Gehry using

Das Guggenheim Museum Bilbao gehört zweifellos zu Frank O. Gehrys sensationellsten Arbeiten. Hier fügen sich die komplexen Formen, mit denen er sich seit vielen Jahren auseinandersetzt (z.B. im noch unausgeführten Entwurf für die Walt Disney Concert Hall in Los Angeles) zu einer phantastisch-plastischen Komposition. Teil eines urbanen Sanierungsprojekts in dieser Industriestadt des Baskenlandes (Kostenpunkt ca. 1,5 Milliarden $), zu dem auch eine neue U-Bahnlinie von Sir Norman Foster gehört sowie eine Fußbrücke und ein Flughafen von Santiago Calatrava, besitzt das Museum 24 000 m² Gesamtfläche, davon 10 600 m² Ausstellungsflächen auf drei Ebenen. Die Exponate des Museums wurden von der Stadt Bilbao, von der Provinz- und der Zentralregierung finanziert, inhaltlich-programmatisch jedoch zu einem Gutteil vom New Yorker Guggenheim ausgewählt, das unter seinem dynamischen Direktor Thomas Krens mehrere Versuche unternommen hat, nach Europa zu expandieren. Das neue Museum ist ein herausragendes städtisches Bauwerk am Ufer des Nervión und wird buchstäblich von der Brücke Puente de la Salve durchkreuzt, die einen Teil der Hauptgalerie überspannt. Von außen betrachtet erscheint die Titanverkleidung der »Metallblumen«-

Le Musée Guggenheim de Bilbao est sans aucun doute l'une des œuvres architecturales les plus spectaculaires de Frank O. Gehry. Ici, les formes complexes qu'il étudie et propose depuis un certain nombre d'années à l'occasion de projets jusqu'à présent non construits, comme le Walt Disney Concert Hall de Los Angeles, composent une symphonie de volumes sculpturaux. Élément d'un projet de rénovation de 9 milliards de F lancé par la ville industrielle du Pays Basque – qui comprend une nouvelle ligne de métro conçue par Sir Norman Foster, une passerelle et un aéroport dessinés par Santiago Calatrava – ce nouveau bâtiment représente une surface totale de 24 000 m², dont 10 600 m² de galeries d'exposition sur trois niveaux. Si le musée a été financé par la ville, la région et l'État espagnol, les collections relèvent pour une bonne part de la responsabilité du Musée Guggenheim de New York qui a déjà tenté plusieurs fois de se développer en Europe, à l'initiative de son dynamique directeur, Thomas Krens. Le nouveau musée est une construction éminemment urbaine, implantée au bord du Nervión, et littéralement traversé par le pont Puente de la Salve qui surplombe une partie de la principale galerie d'exposition. Vue de l'extérieur, l'aspect le plus spectaculaire est le recouvre-

Both drawing and actual images of the structure emphasize its highly sculptural volumes. These forms are all the more surprising in light of the densely urban context into which the museum is set.

Sowohl die Zeichnung als auch Aufnahmen des fertigen Gebäudes heben seine plastischen Formen hervor. Angesichts der dicht bebauten städtischen Umgebung, in die das Museum hineingestellt wurde, wirken diese Formen umso erstaunlicher.

Le dessin comme les photographies du bâtiment achevé mettent en valeur ses volumes sculpturaux. Ces formes sont encore plus surprenantes dans le contexte urbain dense du musée.

Frank O. Gehry: Guggenheim Museum Bilbao, 1991–97 **65**

Although this canopy facing the Nervión River gives
the impression from a distance of being the main
entrance, it is not. Gehry's shapes may spring from
figurative or anthropomorphic associations (a boat or
a dancer), they avoid any hint of literalism.

Auch wenn dieses Vordach zum Nervión hin aus der
Ferne den Eindruck vermittelt, als markiere es den
Haupteingang, ist dem nicht so. Gehrys Formen
entspringen vielleicht figurativen oder anthropomorphen
Vorstellungen (Schiff oder Tänzer), vermeiden aller-
dings jede direkte Abbildung.

Vu de loin, cet auvent qui fait face au Nervión, donne à
tort l'impression d'être l'entrée principale. Si les formes
dessinées par Gehry peuvent entraîner des associations
d'idées figuratives (un bateau, un danseur), elles
ne tombent jamais dans la représentation littérale.

the CATIA program developed by Dassault in France for fighter plane design. On the inside, visitors are greeted by a 55 meter high atrium, which cuts through the heart of the building. There are eighteen galleries, but the most spectacular of these by far is the main exhibition space, which is free of structural columns and measures no less than 130 meters in length and 30 meters in width. Inevitably, such spaces invite comparison to the cathedrals of another era. Gehry also reaches the apogee here of his natural tendency to want to create buildings which are in and of themselves works of art.

Formen als die sensationellste Seite des Bauwerks. Gehry hat sie mit Hilfe des von Dassault, Frankreich, für Kampfflugzeuge entwickelten CATIA-Computerprogramms modelliert. Beim Eintreten werden Besucher von einem 55 m hohen, das Gebäude durchschneidenden Atrium in Empfang genommen. Von den insgesamt 18 Ausstellungshallen ist die Hauptgalerie am eindrucksvollsten: ein stützenfreier Raum von nicht weniger als 130 x 30 m, der unvermeidlich zu Vergleichen mit den Kathedralen anderer Epochen auffordert. Gehry erreichte auch hier sein stets angestrebtes Ziel, Gebäude zu schaffen, die an und für sich ein Kunstwerk sind, und zwar in höchster Vollendung.

ment en titane de sa «fleur métallique», dont les formes ont été modelées par Gehry à l'aide du logiciel CATIA mis au point en France par Dassault pour la conception d'avions de chasse. À l'intérieur, les visiteurs sont accueillis dans un atrium de 55 m de haut, découpé au cœur du bâtiment. Il contient 18 galeries, dont la plus spectaculaire est l'espace principal d'exposition, libre de toute colonne de soutien et qui mesure pas moins de 130 m de long sur 30 m de large. Inévitablement, de tels espaces invitent à la comparaison avec les cathédrales du passé. Gehry atteint ici à l'apogée de sa tendance naturelle à créer des bâtiments qui sont eux-mêmes des œuvres d'art.

Page 68: The museum entrance.
Page 69: Images of the interior with its complex forms, and a work by Claes Oldenburg, commissioned for the Guggenheim Museum Bilbao.

Seite 68: Der Haupteingang des Museums.
Seite 69: Innenaufnahmen zeigen die komplexen Bauformen und die Skulptur von Claes Oldenburg, eine Auftragsarbeit für das Guggenheim Museum Bilbao.

Page 68: L'entrée du musée.
Page 69: Vues de l'intérieur aux formes complexes, et d'une œuvre de Claes Oldenburg, spécialement commandée pour le Musée Guggenheim de Bilbao.

The titanium cladding of the museum takes on different coloring according to lighting conditions. This fact, together with its exuberant forms, make its presence anything but static in the industrial landscape of central Bilbao.

Die Fassadenverkleidung aus Titanplatten nimmt je nach Lichtverhältnis verschiedene Farbnuancen an. Das Museum wirkt also im Gewerbegebiet im Zentrum Bilbaos nicht nur aufgrund seiner überschwenglichen Formen alles andere als statisch.

Le titane qui recouvre l'extérieur change de couleur en fonction de la lumière du jour, ce qui rend la présence du musée dans le paysage industriel et urbain du centre de Bilbao encore plus dynamique.

Pages 72–73: The unusually complex configuration of the exterior volumes of the Guggenheim Bilbao was made possible through the use of Dassault's CATIA program. Exterior and interior attain a kind of organic rapport.

Pages 74–75: The soaring volumes of the atrium contain skirt-like shapes that bring to mind Gehry's work at the American Center in Paris or in the facade of the Nationale Nederlanden Building in Prague.

Seite 72–73: Die ungewöhnlich komplexe äußere Form des Museums konnte mit Hilfe von Dassaults CATIA-Computerprogramm realisiert werden. Außenhülle und Innenraum erreichen sozusagen eine organische Beziehung.

Seite 74–75: Das hoch aufragende Atrium enthält damenrock-ähnliche Elemente, die an Gehrys American Center in Paris oder Teile der Fassade des Nationale Nederlanden-Gebäudes in Prag denken lassen.

Pages 72–73: La configuration inhabituellement complexe des volumes extérieurs du Musée Guggenheim de Bilbao a été rendue en grande partie possible par le logiciel CATIA de Dassault. L'extérieur et l'intérieur entretiennent une sorte de rapport organique.

Pages 74–75: Les volumes élancés de l'atrium contiennent des formes «en jupe» qui font penser à l'American Center construit à Paris par Gehry, ou à la façade de l'immeuble Nationale Nederlanden à Prague.

Frank O. Gehry: Guggenheim Museum Bilbao, 1991–97 **73**

The main exhibition space is no less than 130 meters in length. Although this curving gallery may not be suited to all types of art, it does hold the shape of a very large work by Richard Serra commissioned for the museum very well.

Die Hauptausstellungshalle ist 130 m lang und geschwungen. Auch wenn sie vielleicht nicht für alle Kunstwerke geeignet ist, kommt darin eine riesige Skulptur von Richard Serra – eine Auftragsarbeit für das Museum – sehr gut zur Geltung.

Le principal espace d'exposition ne mesure pas moins de 130 m de long. Si cette galerie en courbe ne se prête pas à toutes les formes d'art, elle accueille avec aisance une œuvre de grande envergure de Richard Serra, commandée par le musée.

76 Frank O. Gehry: Guggenheim Museum Bilbao, 1991–97

Nationale Nederlanden Building,
Rasin Embankment
Prague, Czech Republic, 1992–1996

Nicknamed "Fred and Ginger" by Prague residents, this building, which measures some 5,842 square meters, is located near the banks of the Vltava River on one of only three sites in the historic district of the city where new construction has been allowed. Made of precast concrete panels with a plaster finish to fit in somewhat with local architecture, the building was designed with Dassault's CATIA program, also used for the Guggenheim Museum Bilbao, and with Parametric Technology's Pro/Engineer. This system permitted close cost control despite the unusual forms of the structure. Gehry's own statement about the building underlines his concern with the historic context, but, inevitably, such an unusual building sparked some controversy. The young Prague architect Zdenek Jiran most notably took Gehry to task for "irresponsible exhibitionism." Paul Koch of the Nationale Nederlanden group was involved in the choice of Frank O. Gehry for this building, much as he has been in other interesting architectural initiatives in Eastern Europe, such as the ING Bank building renovation carried out by Erick van Egeraat in Budapest (1992–94).

Dieses Gebäude (von den Pragern »Fred und Ginger« getauft) mit einer Gesamtfläche von etwa 5 842 m² steht am Ufer der Moldau auf einem von nur drei Grundstücken in der historischen Altstadt von Prag, die zur Neubebauung freigegeben worden waren. Es ist aus vorgefertigten Betonplatten ausgeführt und verputzt, damit es sich in den Altbaubestand einfügt. Gehry entwarf es mit Hilfe des auch für das Guggenheim Museum in Bilbao eingesetzten CATIA-Programms von Dassault sowie mit dem Pro/Engineer-Programm des Software-Entwicklers Parametric Technology. Dieses System ermöglichte trotz der ungewöhnlichen Formen des Bauwerks eine knappe Kostenkalkulation. Gehrys Äußerungen zu seinem Entwurf unterstreichen seine Rücksichtnahme auf den historischen Kontext, aber ein derart ungewöhnliches Gebäude gab natürlich auch Anlaß zu kontroverser Diskussion. Der junge Prager Architekt Zdenek Jiran warf Gehry zum Beispiel »unverantwortlichen Exhibitionismus« vor. Paul Koch von der Nationale Nederlanden-Gruppe war mitverantwortlich für die Wahl Gehrys als Architekt, ebenso wie für einige andere interessante Architektur-Initiativen in Osteuropa – etwa die Restaurierung und den Umbau des ING Bankgebäudes in Budapest durch Erick van Egeraat (1992–94).

Surnommé «Ginger and Fred» par les Praguois, cet immeuble de 5 842 m² se trouve en bordure de la Moldau, sur l'un des trois seuls terrains du centre historique de la ville où il était encore possible de construire à neuf. Les plans ont été réalisés avec l'aide des logiciels CATIA de l'entreprise Dassault, également utilisés pour le Musée Guggenheim de Bilbao, et Pro/Engineer, de Parametric Technology. Ce système permet un contrôle précis des coûts, malgré les formes très inhabituelles de la construction. Les façades en panneaux de béton préfabriqués recouverts de plâtre tentent de s'harmoniser à l'environnement. Certaines déclarations de Gehry soulignent son souci du contexte historique, mais l'immeuble n'en a pas moins soulevé quelques controverses. Le jeune architecte praguois Zdenek Jiran, en particulier, a pris à parti Gehry pour son «exhibitionnisme irresponsable». Paul Koch du Groupe Nationale-Nederlanden a participé au choix de l'architecte californien pour cet immeuble, ainsi qu'à d'autres initiatives architecturales intéressantes en Europe centrale, comme la rénovation de l'immeuble de la banque ING de Budapest, confiée à Erick van Egeraat (1992–94).

The figurative and kinetic nature of Gehry's design is fully evident to the right. A "dress" or "skirt" made of glass reveals the supporting columns.

Der figurative und kinetische Charakter von Gehrys Entwurf wird rechts im Bild ganz augenfällig. Ein »Kleid« oder »Damenrock« aus Glas läßt die tragenden Säulen durchscheinen.

La nature figurative et cinétique du travail de Gehry s'affirme dans la photographie de droite. Une «robe» ou «jupe» de verre masque en partie les colonnes de soutien.

Despite some local criticism, the Nationale Nederlanden Building does make numerous concessions to its architectural environment, including the facade alignments along the river bank.

Das Gebäude der Nationale Nederlanden macht zahlreiche Konzessionen an seine bauliche Umgebung, einschließlich der Fassadenausrichtung parallel zum Flußufer.

Malgré quelques critiques locales, l'immeuble Nationale Nederlanden fait de nombreuses concessions à son environnement architectural, dont l'alignement de ses façades le long du quai.

Frank O. Gehry: Nationale Nederlanden Building, 1992–96 **81**

The sculptural forms favored by Frank O. Gehry are fully evident in this image, as is the contrast between the upright "Fred" form and the more curvilinear "Ginger" volume near the entrance.

Die von Frank O. Gehry bevorzugten plastischen Formen sind auf diesem Bild deutlich zu sehen, ebenso der Kontrast zwischen der aufrechten »Fred«-Figur und der krummlinigen »Ginger«-Form im Bereich des Eingangs.

Les formes sculpturales qu'affectionne Frank O. Gehry prennent tout leur poids dans ces images, ainsi que dans le contraste entre la tour rectiligne, surnommée «Fred», et la partie «Ginger», tout en courbes.

Steven Holl

"A new architecture must be formed that is simultaneously aligned with transcultural continuity and with the poetic expression of individual situations and communities," writes Steven Holl, one of the more promising architects currently working in the United States. Although his approach is often unexpected, as in the "bottles of light" that inspired the Chapel of St. Ignatius published here, Holl's thoughtful analysis of projects, often informed by a rich cultural background, stands out from a good deal of American architecture, which more often than not takes a route of economic expediency. Holl also eschews a media-oriented approach, which means that he is less wellknown than some of his colleagues. Undoubtedly, with the completion of projects like the new Museum of Contemporary Art in Helsinki, his work will be recognized more widely for its substantive originality and modern spirit. Current work also includes the Cranbrook Institute of Science, Bloomfield Hills, Michigan (1998).

»Wir müssen eine neue Architektur schaffen, die einhergeht mit transkultureller Kontinuität und zugleich mit dem poetischen Ausdruck individueller Situationen und Gemeinschaften«, schreibt Steven Holl, ein vielversprechender jüngerer US-amerikanischer Architekt. Da er in oft unerwarteter Weise an eine Bauaufgabe herangeht, was die »Lichtflaschen« der hier vorgestellten St. Ignatius-Kapelle belegen, heben sich Holls Arbeiten (häufig durchdrungen von vielfältigen Kultureinflüssen) von einem Großteil der amerikanischen Architektur ab, die meist den Weg ökonomischer Zweckdienlichkeit geht. Holl verweigert sich zudem einem medien-orientierten Ansatz, und deshalb ist er weniger bekannt als einige seiner Kollegen. Mit der Vollendung von Bauten wie dem Museum für Gegenwartskunst in Helsinki wird seine höchst originelle und fortschrittliche Architektur zweifellos größere Beachtung finden. Zu Holls neuesten Projekten gehört das Cranbrook Institute of Science, Bloomfield Hills, Michigan (1998).

«Nous attendons une nouvelle architecture qui soit simultanément d'inspiration transculturelle et prenne en compte l'expression poétique des situations individuelles et des groupes humains», écrit Steven Holl, l'un des architectes américains les plus prometteurs. Bien que son approche soit souvent inattendue, comme dans ces «bouteilles de lumière» qui lui ont inspiré la chapelle de Saint-Ignace présentée ici, l'analyse soignée qu'il fait de ses projets, souvent nourrie d'une connaissance approfondie du contexte culturel, se distingue nettement d'une architecture américaine qui, plus souvent qu'il ne le faudrait, préfère la voie de l'efficacité économique. Holl se tient par ailleurs à l'écart de toute médiatisation, ce qui explique qu'il soit moins célèbre que certains de ses collègues. Mais avec l'achèvement de projets comme le nouveau musée d'art contemporain d'Helsinki, son œuvre sera sans aucun doute enfin mieux reconnue, pour son originalité substantielle et sa modernité. Il travaille également en ce moment sur le projet du Cranbrook Institute of Science, Bloomfield Hills, Michigan (1998).

Steven Holl, Chapel of St. Ignatius, Seattle University, Seattle, Washington, 1994–97.

Steven Holl, St. Ignatius-Kapelle, Seattle University, Seattle, Washington, 1994–97.

Steven Holl, Chapelle Saint-Ignace, Université de Seattle, Washington, 1994–97.

Chapel of St. Ignatius, Seattle University

Seattle, Washington, 1994–1997

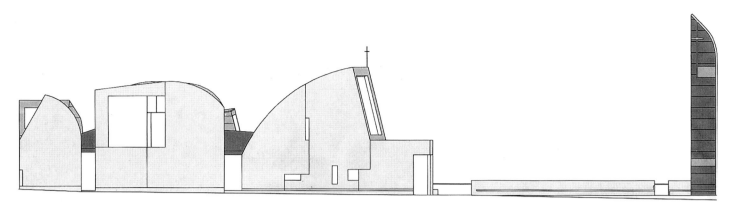

Built on a limited budget, this 5,800 square meter chapel was designed by Steven Holl on the basis of a design concept in which he placed "bottles of light" in a stone box. Each of these bottles is intended to correspond to an aspect of Catholic worship or of the missions of the Jesuits. Since stained glass was deemed too expensive, the architect worked with a "series of color fields with back-painted baffles and a single piece of stained glass of a complementary color set in the midst of each." Again for cost reasons, the walls are "tilt-up concrete" rather than stone. Steven Holl points out that this process was used by Rudolf Schindler for his Kings Road House in Los Angeles. The roofs are made with "steel tubes bent by magnetic induction through a computer-driven process." The same process was used by Holl in his Stretto House in Dallas. Although the form of the building is elongated for reasons related to the site and the university campus, the seating within is "semicircular, like a chapel in the round."

Für diese 5 800 m² umfassende Kapelle stand nur ein knappes Budget zur Verfügung. Beim Entwurf ging Steven Holl von der Vorstellung von »Lichtflaschen« in einem Steinkasten aus. Jede dieser Flaschen soll einem Teil der katholischen Messe oder der geistlichen Mission der Jesuiten entsprechen. Da Buntglasfenster zu kostspielig gewesen wären, arbeitete der Architekt mit einer Reihe von »Farbfeldern mit hintermalten Ablenkblechen und einem einzelnen Stück Buntglas in der Mitte jedes Feldes«. Aus Kostengründen bestehen die Außenmauern aus Beton anstelle von Naturstein. Steven Holl hat darauf hingewiesen, daß Rudolf Schindler dieses Verfahren auch bei seinem Kings Road House in Los Angeles angewandt hat. Die Dächer sind aus Stahlröhren gefertigt, die »mittels einer computergesteuerten magnetischen Induktion ihre gebogene Form erhielten«. Das gleiche Verfahren setzte Holl bei seinem Stretto House in Dallas ein. Obwohl das Gebäude in bezug auf den Baugrund und die Gegebenheiten des Universitäts-Campus eine längliche Form hat, sind die Sitze innen »im Halbrund [angeordnet], wie in einer Rundkapelle«.

Construite pour un budget limité, cette chapelle de 5 800 m² a été dessinée par Steven Holl sur la base d'un concept de «bouteilles de lumière» dans une boîte de pierre. Chacune de ces «bouteilles» est censée correspondre à un aspect de la foi catholique ou des missions des jésuites. Comme les vitraux étaient trop coûteux, l'architecte a travaillé avec «une série de champs lumineux à cloisons-déflecteurs, peints en partie arrière, avec un seul et unique morceau de verre de couleur complémentaire au milieu de chacun». Toujours pour des raisons financières, les murs sont en béton relevé plutôt qu'en pierre. Steven Holl fait remarquer que ce procédé a été utilisé par Rudolf Schindler dans sa Kings Road House à Los Angeles. Les toits sont en «tubes d'acier courbés par induction magnétique, pilotée par ordinateur». Le même processus a été utilisé par Holl pour sa Stretto House à Dallas. Bien que la forme du bâtiment soit allongée pour des raisons tenant au terrain et au campus de l'université, la disposition des sièges est «semi-circulaire, comme dans une chapelle ronde».

Page 86: The West evelation of the chapel shows its division into nearly distinct volumes.
Page 87: The entrance of the chapel.

Page 86: Die Westansicht der Kapelle zeigt deren Teilung in fast getrennte Bauvolumen.
Page 87: Der Eingang der Kapelle.

Page 86: L'élévation ouest de la chapelle montre sa division en volumes presque distincts.
Page 87: L'entrée de la chapelle.

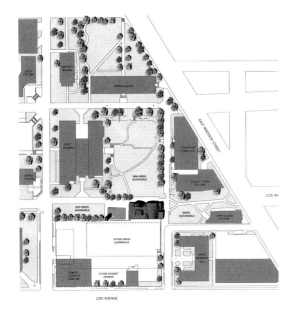

Page 88: The plan and the overall photo show that a "future green quadrangle" is to replace the existing parking lot.
Page 89: The reflecting pool and tower amplify the spatial presence of the chapel.

Seite 88: Lageplan und Gesamtansicht zeigen, daß ein begrünter Hof den bestehenden Parkplatz ersetzen wird.
Seite 89: Die reflektierende Wasserfläche und der Turm steigern die räumliche Präsenz der Kapelle.

Page 88: Le plan et la photo d'ensemble montrent qu'un «futur espace vert carré» devrait remplacer le parking actuel.
Page 89: Le bassin dans lequel se reflète le clocher amplifie la présence spatiale de la chapelle.

Despite the relatively complex manipulations of space
and light introduced by the architect, the whole retains
an air of simplicity that is undoubtedly propitious to
worship and contemplation. A sketch by Steven Holl
demonstrates the principle of "bottles of light," which
he used in the early design phases.

Trotz relativ komplexer Raum- und Licht-Manipulatio-
nen vermittelt der gesamte Innenraum ein Gefühl von
Schlichtheit, was dem Gottesdienst und der Kontem-
plation nur förderlich sein kann. Eine Skizze von Steven
Holl verdeutlicht das Prinzip der »Lichtflaschen«, das
er in der frühen Entwurfsphase verfolgte.

Malgré les manipulations relativement complexes de
l'espace et de la lumière pratiquées par l'architecte,
l'ensemble possède une simplicité propice à la liturgie
et à la contemplation. Un dessin de Steven Holl illustre
le concept de «bouteilles de lumière», dont il est parti.

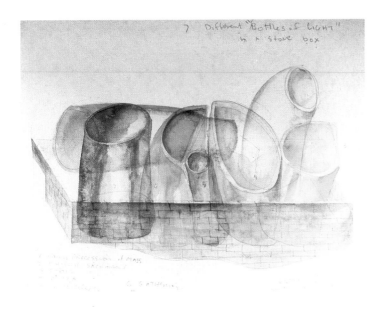

Richard Meier

A member of the "New York Five," Richard Meier has been an architect whose consistent, some would even say obsessional, use of Modernist white forms has become a universally recognizable signature style. Influenced by Le Corbusier, Meier has proven that a gridded, geometrical vocabulary is capable of an astonishing variety of types of expression. Initially on a small scale, for numerous private residences, and later in progessively larger commissions, office buildings, museums or housing, he has evolved toward more complex floor plans, and a shifting of axes that has come to be considered typical of much contemporary architecture. With projects like The Hague City Hall and the new Getty Center, Richard Meier has reached the summit of his profession, both in Europe and in the United States. Current work includes U.S. Courthouse and Federal Building facilities in Phoenix, Arizona and Islip, New York.

Richard Meiers konsequente (manche würden sagen besessene) Verwendung weißer Bauformen nach dem Vorbild des Modernen Bauens gilt als das Markenzeichen dieses Architekten, einem Mitglied der »New York Five«. Der von Le Corbusier beeinflußte Architekt hat bewiesen, daß auch gerasterte geometrische Bauten vielfältige Ausdrucksmöglichkeiten bieten. Anfänglich in kleineren Projekten, vor allem Einfamilienhäusern, später in größeren Bauten wie Bürogebäuden, Museen oder Wohnanlagen, entwickelte Meier immer komplexere Grundrisse und Achsenverschiebungen, die heute für viele Beispiele zeitgenössischer Architektur typisch sind. Mit Bauten wie dem Rathaus von Den Haag und dem neuen Getty Center in Los Angeles ist Meier auf dem Gipfel seiner Karriere angelangt, in Europa wie in Amerika. Laufende Projekte sind u.a. das US Courthouse und Bundesbauten in Phoenix, Arizona sowie Islip, New York.

Membre des «New York Five», Richard Meier est un architecte dont le recours récurrent – certains diront obsessionnel – à un vocabulaire formel d'esprit moderniste est devenu la signature connue dans le monde entier. Influencé par Le Corbusier, Meier a prouvé qu'un vocabulaire géométrique appuyé sur une trame pouvait déboucher sur une étonnante variété d'expressions. Travaillant initialement sur de petits projets pour de nombreuses résidences privées, et plus tard sur des commandes de plus en plus importantes, bureaux, musées et maisons privées, il a évolué vers une plus grande complexité des plans et le pivotement d'axes typique de nombreuses œuvres architecturales contemporaines. Avec des projets comme l'hôtel de ville de La Haye et le nouveau Getty Center, Richard Meier a atteint les sommets de sa profession, aussi bien en Europe qu'aux États-Unis. Il travaille actuellement à des projets pour la Cour de justice fédérale et des immeubles fédéraux à Phoenix, en Arizona, et à Islip, État de New York.

Richard Meier, Getty Center, Los Angeles, California, 1984–97.

Richard Meier, Getty Center, Los Angeles, Kalifornien, 1984–97.

Richard Meier, Getty Center, Los Angeles, Californie, 1984–97.

Getty Center
Los Angeles, California, 1984–1997

Pages 94–95: *The tram station at the bottom of the hill, an overall site plan, and an image of the Getty Trust building within the complex.*
Pages 96–97: *The inner circumference of the Getty Research Institute, a kind of inward looking reply to the drum shape of the entrance atrium of the Museum. Its round shape also bears a clear relation to that of the nearby garden designed by the artist Robert Irwin.*

In many respects, this is the most prestigious commission accorded to an American architect in the final quarter of the 20th century. Set on a spectacular 44.5 hectare hilltop site near the Brentwood area of Los Angeles, it is an 88,000 square meter six building-complex, which groups together the activities of the Getty Trust, including a museum. Richard Meier himself has compared the Center to an Italian hilltop town, and the use of a rugged cleft travertine for much of the cladding does give the whole a much warmer or more Mediterranean feeling than the pure white buildings for which Meier is best known. The Mediterranean image is also appropriate to the circulation established between the buildings – flowered courtyards and open walkways give the whole a congenial atmosphere that is unlike the rather mathematical precision that often characterizes Meier's work. An unexpected note is added in the Museum interiors, where Thierry Despont was responsible for giving a markedly traditional air to the galleries. "In my mind's eye I see a classic structure, elegant and timeless, emerging,

In vielerlei Hinsicht ist das Getty Center das prestigeträchtigste Bauvorhaben, mit dem ein amerikanischer Architekt in den letzten drei Jahrzehnten des 20. Jahrhunderts betraut worden ist. Das Center steht auf einem 44,5 ha großen Hügelgelände in Brentwood, Los Angeles, in herrlicher Lage – ein Ensemble aus sechs Gebäuden mit einer Gesamtfläche von 88 000 m², zu dem auch ein Museum gehört. Richard Meier hat das Center mit einem italienischen Bergstädtchen verglichen, und der für viele Fassadenteile verwendete ungeschliffene Travertin verleiht dem Ensemble tatsächlich mediterranes Flair und mehr Wärme als die weißen Paneele, für die Meier bekannt ist. Die Mittelmeer-Metaphorik paßt auch zu den Verkehrsflächen und Räumen zwischen den einzelnen Gebäuden: Mit blühenden Gewächsen bepflanzte Höfe und Wege unter freiem Himmel geben dem Ganzen eine zur Geselligkeit anregende Atmosphäre – ganz anders als Meiers typische, von mathematischer Präzision gekennzeichnete Bauten. Die Innenräume des Museums überraschen mit ihrer von Thierry Despont gestalteten

À de nombreux égards, le Getty Center est la plus prestigieuse commande passée à un architecte américain au cours de ce dernier quart de siècle. Situé sur un terrain spectaculaire au sommet d'une colline de Brentwood (44,5 hectares), à Los Angeles, il s'agit d'un ensemble de six bâtiments de 88 000 m² qui regroupe toutes les activités du Getty Trust, dont le musée. Richard Meier lui-même a comparé le Centre à un village italien dans les collines, et l'utilisation d'un travertin rugueux pour la plus grande partie du revêtement des murs donne à l'ensemble une allure plus chaleureuse, voire plus méditerranéenne que les grandes surfaces blanches habituellement associées au nom de l'architecte. L'image méditerranéenne correspond également aux circulations créées entre les bâtiments – cours fleuries et passages ouverts – qui donnent une atmosphère de communauté assez différente de la précision quasi mathématique des créations précédentes de Meier. Une note supplémentaire inattendue est fournie par les intérieurs du musée, dont Thierry Despont a été chargé, qui donnent un style résolument

Seite 94–95: Die Straßenbahnhaltestelle am Fuße des Hügels, ein Geländeplan sowie eine Ansicht des Getty Trust-Gebäudes.

Seite 96–97: Das Getty Research Institute – in der Form eine Art Erwiderung auf die Tonnenform des Eingangs-Atriums im Getty Museum. Die Rundform nimmt ebenfalls deutlich Bezug auf den vom Künstler Robert Irwin gestalteten nahegelegenen Garten.

Pages 94–95: La gare de tram au pied de la colline, vue du plan général du site et de l'immeuble du Getty Trust.

Pages 96–97: La salle circulaire du Getty Research Institute renvoie une sorte d'écho intérieur à l'atrium d'entrée du musée, en forme de tambour. Sa rotondité est également conçue en relation avec le jardin dessiné, non loin de là, par l'artiste Robert Irwin.

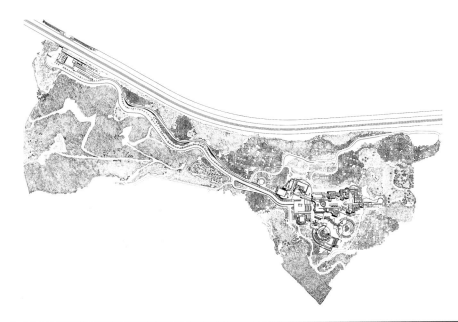

Richard Meier: Getty Center, 1984–97 **95**

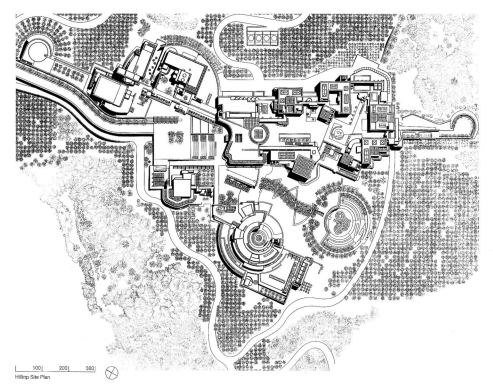

```
100|   200|   300|
Hilltop Site Plan
```

serene and ideal, from the rough hillside, a
kind of Aristotelian structure within the landscape," said the architect some years ago. It is
indeed this rather classical image that prevails
in the Getty Center, a group of buildings that
were plainly built with posterity in mind. Their
very solidity is somehow removed from the
ephemeral architecture of most of Los
Angeles, as is the decidedly European tone of
the collections and the Center itself. The Getty
Center may be too complex in its layout for
some, too much of an exercise in architectural
virtuosity, a problem that has been evident
in some other Meier buildings. It is hard to
classify as a Modernist, Postmodern or
Neo-Modern work, for it is none of these.
It is in a class apart, because of its billion
dollar budget, but also because of its cultural
functions and the ambitions of its directors.

deutlich traditionellen Ausstattung. »Vor
meinem inneren Auge sehe ich einen klassischen Bau, elegant und zeitlos, der sich heiter
und in idealer Form aus dem felsigen Hügel
erhebt, eine Art Aristotelischer Konstruktion in
der Landschaft«, so Meier vor einigen Jahren.
Tatsächlich mutet das Center überwiegend
wie ein relativ klassisches Stück Architektur
an; es ist augenfällig für die Nachwelt gebaut
worden. Die Solidität der Gebäude setzt sich
von der vielfach »ephemeren« Architektur
in Los Angeles ab und entspricht damit der
entschieden europäischen Ausrichtung der
Sammlungen und des Centers selbst. Der
Lageplan des Getty Center ist für manche
vielleicht allzu komplex, zu sehr eine Übung in
architektonischer Virtuosität – ein Problem,
das auch bei etlichen anderen Meier-Entwürfen
besteht. Man kann es weder als modern, postmodern noch als neo-modern bezeichnen,
denn es bildet eine Klasse für sich, einerseits
infolge seines Milliarden-Budgets, andererseits
aufgrund seiner humanistischen Bildungs-
aufgabe und der Ambitioniertheit seiner
Direktoren.

traditionnel aux galeries. «Je vois une structure
classique, élégante et intemporelle, émergeant,
sereine et idéale, du flanc sauvage de la colline,
sorte de structure aristotélicienne dans le
paysage», a déclaré l'architecte il y a quelques
années. C'est en effet cette image classique
qui prévaut dans ce groupe de bâtiments construits en pensant à la postérité. Leur solidité
même est pour une bonne mesure éloignée
du caractère éphémère de l'essentiel de
l'architecture de Los Angeles, de même que la
tonalité décidément européenne des collections et du Centre lui-même. Le Getty Center
est peut-être trop complexe dans son plan,
joue par trop la virtuosité architecturale, problème déjà apparu dans certaines réalisations
antérieures de Meier. Il est difficile de ranger
cet édifice dans la catégorie moderniste,
postmoderniste ou néo-moderniste, car elle
n'appartient réellement à aucune d'entre elles.
Elle est à part, du fait de son budget milliar-
daire en dollars, mais aussi de ses fonctions
culturelles et de l'ambition de ses directeurs.

Meier calls not only on his full vocabulary of architectural forms here, but also on a variety of cladding materials, ranging from his signature white metal panels to beige panels and the ubiquitous cleft travertine.

Meier setzt hier nicht nur die ganze Palette seiner architektonischen Formensprache ein, sondern auch verschiedene Baustoffe – von den für ihn typischen weißen bis zu beigefarbenen Metallpaneelen und ungeschliffenem Travertin.

Ici, Meier fait à la fois appel à la totalité de son vocabulaire formel, mais également à différents matériaux de revêtement, allant de ses célèbres panneaux de métal blanc à des panneaux beige et à un travertin brut omniprésent.

Pages 104–105: The entrance pavilion of the J. Paul Getty Museum gives some idea of the architectural and artistic ambitions of this complex.
Pages 106–107: An image of the museum entrance hall, with its contrast between the white, geometric forms Meier has always preferred and the more unexpected roughness of a cleft travertine wall, faces a reflection of the museum's inner courtyard.

Seite 104–105: Der Eingangsbau zum J. Paul Getty Museum vermittelt einen Eindruck von den architektonischen und künstlerischen Ambitionen dieses Bauprojekts.
Seite 106–107: Ansicht der Eingangshalle des Getty Museums mit den von Meier stets bevorzugten weißen geometrischen Baukörpern im eher unerwarteten Kontrast zur rauhen Oberfläche der abgespalteten Travertinplatten; demgegenüber ein Spiegelbild des Museumsinnenhofes.

Pages 104–105: Le pavillon d'entrée du J. Paul Getty Museum affiche les ambitions architecturales et artistiques de ce complexe.
Pages 106–107: Le hall d'entrée du musée, dont les formes blanches et géométriques ordinairement favorisées par Meier contrastent avec la brutalité encore plus inattendue d'un mur en travertin rugueux. À droite, le reflet de la cour intérieure du musée.

Pages 108–109: The courtyard of the museum.
Page 110: A view of the Gallery of French Decorative Arts (1750–60). The French architect Thierry Despont was responsible for the interior design in this area.
Page 111: A passageway in the museum opens out onto a vista of Los Angeles.

Seite 108–109: Der Innenhof des Museums.
Seite 110: Blick in die Galerie für angewandte Kunst aus Frankreich aus der Zeit von 1750 bis 1760. Der französische Architekt Thierry Despont entwarf die Innenausstattung.
Seite 111: Eine Passage im Museum eröffnet einen Ausblick über Los Angeles.

Pages 108–109: La cour du musée.
Page 110: Vue de la galerie des arts décoratifs français (1750–60). L'architecte français Thierry Despont a été chargé de l'aménagement intérieur de cette partie.
Page 111: L'un des passages du musée s'ouvre sur une vue de Los Angeles.

Rachofsky House
Dallas, Texas, 1991–1996

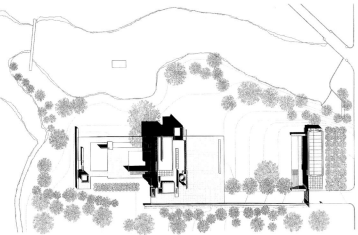

This 1,000 square meter structure is the first residence completed by Richard Meier since the 1980s. Built for a single owner, "The Rachofsky House," as the architect says, "represents an ideal, an investigation into all the possibilities of house as a building type, without many of the usual compromises. In this sense, I suppose, the Rachofsky House is a case study, inducing us to look at and think about what our own notions of house and home encompass." Richard Meier had already designed a house for the same client in the 1980s, but that project was never built, in part because the client wanted more space for works of art, a feature that is clearly present in the new house. Just as he is completing the Getty Center in Los Angeles, Richard Meier shows that he is just as much attached as ever to the symphonic play of pure white geometric volumes for which he is best known. Where the Getty blends with its environment, the Rachofsky House sits on its site like a perfect object, a modernist sculpture that happens to be a house.

Dieses Haus mit 1000 m² Wohnfläche ist Richard Meiers erstes Einfamilienhaus seit den 80er Jahren. »Das Rachofsky House«, so der Architekt, »stellt ein Ideal dar, es sucht sämtliche Möglichkeiten des Einfamilienhauses als Gebäudetyp auszuschöpfen ohne die üblichen Kompromisse. In diesem Sinne ist es wohl eine Fallstudie, die uns dazu veranlaßt, genau hinzuschauen und zu überlegen, was unsere eigenen Vorstellungen über Haus und Heim eigentlich alles beinhalten.« Schon in den 80ern hatte Richard Meier für den gleichen Auftraggeber ein Haus entworfen, das jedoch nie gebaut wurde, unter anderem, weil der Bauherr sich mehr Platz für seine Kunstsammlung wünschte. Dieser ist nun im neuen Haus vorhanden. Während er an der Fertigstellung des Getty Center in Los Angeles arbeitete, bewies Meier mit dem Rachofsky House, daß er wie eh und je am symphonischen Zusammenspiel rein-weißer Baukörper festhält, für das er am besten bekannt ist. Das Getty Center fügt sich in seine Umgebung ein, das Rachofsky House steht dagegen auf seinem Grundstück wie ein perfektes Kunstobjekt, eine moderne Skulptur, die zufällig ein Wohnhaus ist.

Cette construction de 1000 m² est la première résidence privée réalisée par Richard Meier depuis les années 80. Construite pour M. Rachofsky, elle représente, comme le précise l'architecte, «un idéal, une exploration de toutes les possibilités d'une maison en tant que type de construction, sans la plupart des compromis habituels. En ce sens, je suppose, la Rachofsky House est une étude de cas, qui conduit à une remise en cause de ce que recouvrent nos propres notions de maison et de foyer.» Richard Meier avait déjà étudié une résidence pour le même client dans les années 80, mais le projet était resté sur plans, en partie parce que le propriétaire souhaitait davantage de place pour ses œuvres d'art, ce qu'il a à l'évidence obtenu dans cette nouvelle version. Alors qu'il achève le Getty Center, Richard Meier montre qu'il reste attaché comme toujours à la symphonie des purs volumes géométriques qui l'ont rendu célèbre. Si le Getty Center se fond dans son environnement, la Rachofsky House se dresse sur son site telle un objet parfait, aussi bien une sculpture moderniste qu'une maison privée.

As is the case in many of his private houses, and indeed in much of his architecture, Meier closes one facade for privacy, while opening the opposite one to offer open views, but also to bring ample light to the interior.

Wie bei vielen seiner Einfamilienhäuser und überhaupt in seinem ganzen Œuvre schließt Meier eine Fassade, um die Privatsphäre abzuschirmen, während er die gegenüberliegende Außenwand öffnet, um Ausblicke zu schaffen und Licht ins Innere zu bringen.

Comme dans beaucoup de ses résidences particulières, et dans la plupart de ses réalisations, Meier referme une façade pour créer un sentiment d'intimité, et ouvre totalement l'autre pour créer des vues, et apporter le maximum de lumière à l'intérieur.

An earlier concept for the same client was rejected
partially because there was not enough space for the
art collection. Here the orchestration of volumes,
which might recall a cubist composition, makes room
for paintings.

Der Bauherr hatte einen früheren Entwurf abgelehnt,
zum Teil, weil er nicht genug Raum für seine Kunstsammlung geboten hätte. Hier schafft die »Orchestrie-
rung« der Raumvolumen, die an eine kubistische
Komposition erinnert, Wandflächen für das Aufhängen
von Gemälden.

Une première proposition pour le même client fut
en partie rejetée parce qu'elle ne prévoyait pas assez
de place pour la collection d'œuvres d'art. Ici, l'orchestration des volumes, qui évoque une composition
cubiste, laisse la place nécessaire aux peintures.

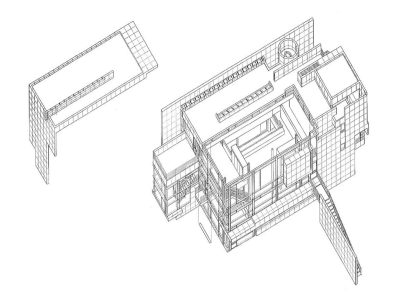

Richard Meier: Rachofsky House, 1991–96 **115**

François de Menil

François de Menil does not have a typical architect's background. The son of Dominique and John de Menil, who was the chairman of Schlumberger, he briefly attended Columbia in 1965 before deciding that he would rather be a film maker. He completed films about the sculptors Jean Tinguely, Niki de Saint Phalle, and Mark di Suvero before creating a production company called FDM, which concentrated on Broadway plays. Having grown up in a house designed by Philip Johnson, owning a Richard Neutra house in Los Angeles, and having commissioned a house in East Hampton by Charles Gwathmey, François de Menil was clearly very interested in architecture. In 1987, he obtained a Bachelor of Architecture degree from The Cooper Union and worked in the offices of Richard Meier and Kohn Pederson Fox before founding his own firm in New York in 1991. He has completed numerous boutique designs for Bottega Veneta, in particular in Japan, and offices for Esquire Magazine and Wells/BDDP in New York (1997). François de Menil says that his work "is rooted in a search for an architecture of essence and simplicity that enhances the human spirit." That definition would seem to fit the Byzantine Fresco Chapel Museum published here quite well.

François de Menil, Sohn von Dominique und John de Menil (ehemaliger Vorstandsvorsitzender von Schlumberger), ist auf indirektem Wege Architekt geworden. 1965 gab er nur ein kurzes Gastspiel an der Columbia University, bevor er beschloß, doch lieber Filmemacher zu werden. Er drehte Dokumentarfilme über die Künstler Jean Tinguely, Niki de Saint Phalle und Mark di Suvero und gründete dann die FDM-Produktionsgesellschaft, die Broadway-Stücke produzierte. Er war in einem von Philip Johnson entworfenen Haus aufgewachsen, besaß in Los Angeles ein von Richard Neutra gebautes Haus und hatte ein weiteres in East Hampton bei Charles Gwathmey in Auftrag gegeben. François de Menil interessierte sich also sehr für Architektur, studierte das Fach schließlich an der Cooper Union (B. A. 1987) und arbeitete bei Richard Meier und Kohn Pederson Fox, bevor er 1991 sein eigenes Büro in New York gründete. Er hat zahlreiche Boutiquen für die Kette Bottega Veneta ausgestattet, vor allem in Japan, ebenso Büroräume für Esquire Magazine und Wells/BDDP in New York (1997). Menil sagt über seine Arbeit, sie sei eine »Suche nach einer Architektur des Wesentlichen und der Einfachheit, die den menschlichen Geist beflügelt«. Das trifft ziemlich genau auf seinen Entwurf zum hier publizierten Kapellen-Museum zu.

La formation de François de Menil est loin d'être classique. Fils de Dominique et John de Menil, l'ancien président de Schlumberger, il étudie brièvement à Columbia University en 1965 avant de décider de devenir réalisateur. Il réalise des films sur les sculpteurs Jean Tinguely, Niki de Saint Phalle et Mark di Suvero avant de créer sa société de production, FDM, spécialisée dans les spectacles de Broadway. Ayant grandi dans une maison dessinée par Philip Johnson, possédant une villa de Richard Neutra à Los Angeles, et s'étant fait construire une résidence par Charles Gwathmey à East Hampton, François de Menil s'intéresse évidemment beaucoup à l'architecture. En 1987, il obtient un B.A. en architecture de Cooper Union, et travaille dans les agences de Richard Meier et Kohn Pederson Fox, avant de fonder sa propre agence à New York en 1991. Il a réalisé de nombreuses boutiques pour Bottega Veneta, en particulier au Japon, et des bureaux pour Esquire Magazine et l'agence de publicité Wells/BDDP à New York (1997). Il aime dire que ses projets «prennent racine dans la recherche d'une architecture de l'essence et de la simplicité qui élève l'esprit». Cette définition semble correspondre assez bien à sa chapelle-musée des fresques byzantines.

François de Menil, Byzantine Fresco Chapel Museum, Houston, Texas, 1991–96. A 13th century Byzantine fresco.

François de Menil, Kapellen-Museum für byzantinische Fresken, Houston, Texas, 1991–96. Ein byzantinisches Fresko aus dem 13. Jahrhundert.

François de Menil, chapelle-musée des fresques byzantines, Houston, Texas, 1991–96. Une fresque byzantine datant du XIIIe siècle.

Byzantine Fresco Chapel Museum

Houston, Texas, 1991–1996

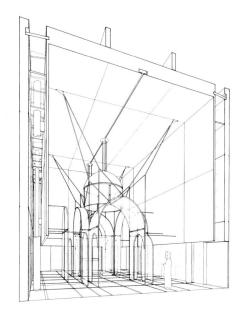

The Byzantine Fresco Chapel Museum in Houston was built to house fragments of 13th century frescoes removed by thieves from the Church of St. Tehmonianos at Lysi on the island of Cyprus. Purchased in 1983 by the Menil Foundation, the works were restored and kept in the United States with the agreement of the Church of Cyprus, since the chapel involved is in Turkish-held territory. Though the frescoes remain the property of the Church of Cyprus they are now exhibited in a structure whose austere exterior is made of precast concrete panels. Within, an effort has been made to evoke the shape of the original chapel, and the placement of the frescoes within that liturgical space. This evocation is accomplished in a most subtle fashion using 2.22 and 3.175 centimeter diameter steel pipes, which trace the form of the chapel, and 3.8 centimeter thick laminated glass sheets to locate the walls. Light from the exterior, washing along the perimeter walls, is contrasted with the black interior of the surrounding structure. Within, the frescoes appear to float in space, while retaining their original spatial relationship.

Das Byzantine Fresco Chapel Museum in Houston wurde gebaut, um darin Fresken des 13. Jahrhunderts unterzubringen, die von Dieben aus der St. Tehmonianos-Kirche in Lysi auf Zypern abgenommen worden waren. Sie wurden 1983 von der Menil Foundation erworben und restauriert. Die Fresken gehören zwar weiterhin der griechisch-orthodoxen Kirche Zyperns, diese stimmte dem Verbleib in den USA aber zu, da sich die Kirche im türkisch besetzten Gebiet der Insel befindet. Als Dauerleihgabe werden sie nun in einem Bau ausgestellt, dessen streng reduzierte Fassaden mit Betontafeln verkleidet sind. Innen hat der Architekt versucht, die Form der zypriotischen Kirche anzudeuten und die ursprüngliche Anordnung der Fresken in jenem Sakralraum wiederherzustellen. Die Umrisse der alten Kirche sind als Gerüst aus Stahlröhren (Durchmesser 2,22 und 3,175 cm) nachempfunden, in das 3,8 cm dicke »Kirchenmauern« aus Mehrscheibensicherheitsglas eingefügt sind. Licht flutet diese Glaswände hinunter, wodurch sich der nachempfundene Kirchenraum in seiner Helligkeit stark vom Dunkel des umgebenden Raums abhebt. Die in ihm aufgehängten Fresken scheinen im Raum zu schweben, während sie ihre ursprünglichen räumlichen Bezüge beibehalten.

La chapelle-musée des fresques byzantines à Houston a été construite pour abriter des fragments de fresques du XIIIᵉ siècle sauvées des voleurs dans l'église chypriote de Saint-Tehmonianos à Lysi. Achetées en 1983 par la Menil Foundation, ces œuvres ont été restaurées et sont conservées aux États-Unis avec l'accord de l'Église de Chypre, car la chapelle d'origine se trouve en zone turque. Les fresques, qui restent la propriété de l'Église chypriote, sont maintenant exposées dans une construction dont l'extérieur austère a été érigé en panneaux de béton préfabriqué. À l'intérieur, un effort a été fait pour évoquer la forme de la chapelle grecque et le placement des fresques par rapport à cet espace liturgique. Cette évocation est mise en œuvre de manière très subtile, à l'aide de tubes d'acier de 2,22 et 3,175 cm de diamètre qui retracent la forme de la chapelle, et des panneaux de verre laminé de 3,8 cm d'épaisseur qui rappellent les murs. La lumière extérieure qui balaye les murs périmétriques contraste avec l'intérieur sombre de la structure environnante. À l'intérieur de celle-ci, les fresques semblent flotter dans l'espace, tout en conservant leur position et leurs relations spatiales d'origine.

The exterior of the Museum is deceptively simple, or even austere, perhaps recalling some of the designs of the Japanese architect Tadao Ando. A sketch and a drawing (above) show how the form of the original chapel is suggested within this volume.

Die äußere Form des Museums ist täuschend schlicht, ja sogar karg, und erinnert vielleicht an einige Bauten des Japaners Tadao Ando. Eine Skizze und eine Zeichnung (oben) zeigen, wie die Form der kleinen, alten Kirche im Innenraum angedeutet wird.

L'extérieur du musée affiche une simplicité, voire une austérité trompeuses qui évoquent certains dessins de l'architecte japonais Tadao Ando. Une esquisse et un dessin (en haut) montrent la manière dont la forme de la chapelle originale est suggérée à l'intérieur de ce volume.

François de Menil: Byzantine Fresco Chapel Museum, 1991–96 **119**

Within the structure, the shape of the chapel on Cyprus
from which the frescoes came is evoked through the use
of steel tubing and frosted glass.

Die Umrisse der kleinen Kirche auf Zypern, woher
die Fresken stammen, sind – in Stahlrohr und Milchglas
ausgeführt – in den Innenraum eingestellt.

À l'intérieur, la forme de la chapelle chypriote d'où
proviennent les fresques est évoquée par des tubes
d'acier et des panneaux de verre givré.

Sambo Mockbee
and the Rural Studio

Each year, the architect Samuel Mockbee, who is a professor at Auburn University, brings twelve students from Auburn to Greensboro, Alabama, where they live in an abandoned antebellum house and design and build houses for the poor living in Hale County. Although the Rural Studio does receive some funding from the Alabama Power Foundation, the projects undertaken by the students are carried out with minimal backing, which means that inexpensive materials are a priority. Substantial efforts are made to design houses which take into account not only the local warm climate, but also the lifestyle of the residents, most of whom have spent their lives in sheds or other temporary structures. "Our goal is to help people get what they think they need, and not what we think they need," says Mockbee, who has his own architectural firm, Mockbee/Coker. Approximately ninety students have participated in the Rural Studio project since it was begun in 1993, "looking for something that is real," as Dennis Ruth another professor from Auburn who participates in the project says. As Sambo Mockbee says, "We are doing this in the exact place where James Agee and Walker Evans lived in the 1930s when they documented the miserable truth of the sharecropper's lives in 'Let Us Now Praise Famous Men.' It's not much different now. The needs are so great."

Jedes Jahr nimmt Samuel Mockbee, Professor für Architektur an der Auburn University, zwölf seiner Studenten mit nach Greensboro, Alabama, wo sie in einem leeren Haus aus der Zeit um 1840 wohnen und für die Armen des Hale County Häuser entwerfen und bauen. Das Rural Studio wird zwar von der Alabama Power Foundation unterstützt, ansonsten aber erhalten die Studentenprojekte minimale Fördermittel, so daß der Einsatz billiger Baustoffe zwingend ist. Sie bemühen sich, beim Entwerfen und Bauen der Wohneinheiten nicht nur das warme Klima zu berücksichtigen, sondern auch die »Ansprüche« der Bewohner, von denen die meisten ihr ganzes Leben in irgendwelchen Schuppen gewohnt haben. »Unser Ziel ist es, den Menschen das zu geben, was sie selbst für notwendig halten, und nicht das, von dem wir meinen, daß sie es brauchen«, sagt Mockbee, der sein eigenes Architekturbüro hat, Mockbee/Coker. Etwa 90 Studenten haben seit der Gründung von Rural Studio 1993 an dem Projekt mitgewirkt, weil sie »etwas Reales suchen«, so Dennis Ruth, ebenfalls Professor an der Auburn-Universität und Teilnehmer an diesem Programm. Sambo Mockbee erklärt: »Wir tun diese Arbeit an genau dem Ort, wo James Agee und Walker Evans in den 30er Jahren lebten und die elenden Lebensbedingungen der ›sharecroppers‹ in ›Let Us Now Praise Famous Men‹ dokumentierten. Heute ist es nicht viel anders. Die Not ist groß.«

Chaque année, l'architecte Samuel Mockbee, professeur à Auburn University, emmène douze de ses étudiants à Greensboro, en Alabama, dans une demeure abandonnée datant d'avant la guerre de Sécession, où ils dessinent et construisent des maisons pour les pauvres du comté de Hale. Bien que Rural Studio reçoive quelques subventions de l'Alabama Power Foundation, les projets des étudiants sont réalisés avec le minimum de moyens, d'où la nécessité de trouver des matériaux bon marché. Ils s'efforcent donc de concevoir des maisons qui prennent en compte non seulement la chaleur du climat local, mais également les modes de vie des futurs résidents, dont la plupart n'ont guère connu que des abris ou des structures temporaires. «Notre but est d'aider les gens à accéder à ce dont ils pensent avoir besoin, et non de leur donner ce que nous pensons qu'ils ont besoin,» précise Mockbee qui dirige par ailleurs sa propre agence d'architecture, Mockbee/Coker. Environ 90 étudiants ont participé au projet de Rural Studio depuis ses débuts en 1993. «Nous cherchions alors un projet concret,» explique Dennis Ruth, autre enseignant d'Auburn qui participe à cette action. Sambo Mockbee ajoute également qu'ils travaillent «à l'endroit exact où James Agee et Walker Evans vivaient dans les années 30, lorsqu'ils enquêtaient sur la misère des ouvriers agricoles retracée dans ‹Let Us Now Praise Famous Men›. Les choses ne sont pas très différentes aujourd'hui. Les besoins sont tout aussi grands.»

Sambo Mockbee and the Rural Studio, Bryant House, Mason's Bend, Alabama, 1995–97. The "smokehouse."

Sambo Mockbee mit Rural Studio, Bryant House, Mason's Bend, Alabama, 1995–97. Das »Räucherhaus«.

Sambo Mockbee et le Rural Studio, Bryant House, Mason's Bend, Alabama, 1995–97. Le «fumoir».

Bryant House
Harris House
Yancey Chapel

Mason's Bend, Alabama, 1995–1997

These projects are unusual in almost every aspect. Built without specific plans, with very limited budgets, and with locally available materials, they are not so much examples of an aesthetic approach to architecture, as they are an answer to one of the most significant problems posed to the profession. How can architects improve the life of ordinary people? The Bryant House is an 80 square meter structure made of materials like hay and corrugated acrylic for the "sun-visor." It cost $16,500 to build. The Harris House, a 60 square meter one-bedroom house located close by includes a 20 square meter porch, and has a "butterfly roof" to facilitate natural ventilation. The Yancey Chapel was made from scavenged materials such as tires, rusted I-beams, big trusses, pine from a 100 year old house, sheets of tin from an old barn, and river slate. All three of these structures are a testimony to the desire of the architectural students who built them to help people in need, and to get away from a purely theoretical approach to their profession.

Die drei hier gezeigten Projekte sind in fast jeder Hinsicht ungewöhnlich. Ohne präzise Pläne und mit äußerst knappen Mitteln aus örtlich erhältlichen Materialien errichtet, sind sie nicht so sehr Beispiele für einen ästhetischen Entwurfsansatz, als vielmehr Lösungsvorschläge für eine der schwierigsten Fragen der Architektur: Wie können Architekten dem Normalbürger ein besseres Leben ermöglichen? Das Bryant House mit 80 m² Wohnfläche besteht aus Lehm, Stroh und gewelltem Acryl für den »Sonnenschirm«. Die Baukosten betrugen 16 500 $. Nicht weit davon steht das Harris House mit 60 m² Wohnfläche (nur ein Schlafzimmer). Es besitzt eine 20 m² große Veranda und ein »Schmetterlingsdach« zum Zweck der Luftzirkulation. Die Yancey Chapel entstand aus Schrott, und zwar aus alten Autoreifen, rostigen Doppel-T-Trägern, Balken aus Kiefernholz eines 100 Jahre alten Hauses, Zinkblechen einer alten Scheune und Flußschiefer. Jede dieser drei Konstruktionen resultierte aus dem Wunsch ihrer Erbauer – der Studenten –, Menschen in Not zu helfen und ihren Beruf nicht nur akademisch zu erlernen.

Ces projets sont inhabituels sous pratiquement tous leurs aspects. Construits sans plans spécifiques, à partir de budgets très limités et avec des matériaux disponibles sur place, ils ne sont pas tant des exemples d'une nouvelle approche esthétique de l'architecture qu'une réponse à l'un des problèmes les plus délicats posés à la profession: de quelle façon un architecte peut-il améliorer la vie des gens «ordinaires». Bryant House est une structure de 80 m² construite en matériaux inhabituels, comme du foin et de l'acrylique ondulé pour sa «visière». Elle a coûté 100 000 F. Non loin, Harris House est une maison de deux pièces sur 60 m² qui comprend une véranda de 20 m² et possède un «toit en ailes de papillon» qui facilite la ventilation naturelle. La Yancey Chapel a était édifiée en matériaux de récupération: vieux pneus, IPN rouillés, poutres de pin provenant d'une maison du siècle dernier, feuilles de fer blanc récupérées dans une vieille grange et ardoises de rivière. Ces trois édifices témoignent du désir des étudiants en architecture qui les ont construits d'aider les gens dans le besoin et de se libérer d'une approche purement théorique de leur profession.

Designed without plans in an extremely simple form, the Bryant House nonetheless calls on local materials and traditions, in terms of the lifestyle of the occupants.

Ohne Planzeichnungen in äußerst einfacher Form gestaltet, greift das Bryant House auf örtlich vorhandene Materialien und Traditionen zurück und richtet sich so nach dem Lebensstil der Bewohner.

Conçu sans plans, d'une forme extrêmement simple, la Bryant House n'en fait pas moins appel aux traditions et aux matériaux de la région, tout en s'appuyant sur le mode de vie de ses occupants.

The Harris House features a "butterfly" roof, which facilitates natural ventilation. The openness of the house and the size of its porch are intended to suit the inhabitants and the climate.

Das Harris House hat ein »Schmetterlingsdach«, das eine natürliche Luftbewegung ermöglicht. Die Offenheit des Hauses und die Größe der Veranda passen zum Leben der Bewohner und zum Klima.

Harris House a adopté un toit en «ailes de papillon» qui facilite la ventilation naturelle. L'ouverture de la maison et les dimensions de sa véranda sont adaptés au climat et aux occupants.

Pages 128–131: *Built essentially with scavenged or recuperated materials such as old tires, the Yancey Chapel goes a step beyond the essentially practical implications of the Bryant and Harris houses.*

Seite 128–131: *Die Gestaltung der Yancey Chapel – vorwiegend aus Fundstücken oder wiederverwerteten Materialien erbaut (z.B. alten Autoreifen) – geht über die rein praktischen Entwurfsabsichten für die Häuser Bryant und Harris hinaus.*

Pages 128–131: *Construite essentiellement à partir de matériaux de récupération ou abandonnés – vieux pneus par exemple – la Yancey Chapel marque une avancée par rapport aux préoccupations essentiellement pratiques des maisons Bryant et Harris.*

Thom Mayne

Morphosis

The "modernist penchant for unification and simplification must be broken," writes Morphosis principal Thom Mayne. The work of his group, originally created with Michael Rotondi, has emphasized the importance of societal changes, such as the growing role of electronic communications, and the "breakdown of a conventional notion of community." Although beginning from a different analysis, Morphosis, like certain Japanese architects, has insisted on breaking down the boundaries between the interior and the exterior of buildings. This is clearly the goal in the Blades Residence published here. Since its first projects, Morphosis has placed a great deal of importance on the process that leads after a complex, introspective analysis to construction. Elaborate models have continued to play a role in this transformative investigation.

Die »moderne Neigung zu Vereinheitlichung und Vereinfachung muß gebrochen werden«, schreibt Thom Mayne, Direktor des Architekturbüros Morphosis. Dieses Büro, ursprünglich von Mayne und Michael Rotondi gegründet, betont die Wichtigkeit gesellschaftlicher Veränderungen, etwa die zunehmend wichtiger werdende Rolle elektronischer Kommunikation und den »Zusammenbruch konventioneller Vorstellungen von Gemeinschaft«. Zwar geht Morphosis von einer andersartigen Analyse aus, kommt aber wie einige japanische Architekten zu dem Schluß, daß die Grenzen zwischen Innen- und Außenraum aufgehoben werden müssen. Das war auch ganz klar die Entwurfsabsicht für die hier vorgestellte Blades Residence. Seit Beginn ihrer Tätigkeit hat die Architektengemeinschaft Morphosis dem Prozeß, der nach einer komplexen, introspektiven Analyse zum Bau führt, große Bedeutung beigemessen. Sorgfältig gearbeitete Modelle spielen bei diesen »transformativen Untersuchungen« nach wie vor eine große Rolle.

«Le penchant moderniste à l'unification et à la simplification doit être rejeté», écrit le responsable de Morphosis, Thom Mayne. L'œuvre de ce groupe met l'accent sur l'importance des changements de la société, tels le rôle grandissant de la communication électronique et «l'effondrement de la conception conventionnelle de la vie en commun». Bien que partant d'une analyse différente, Morphosis insiste, comme certains architectes japonais, sur la suppression de la séparation entre l'intérieur et l'extérieur des bâtiments. C'est à l'évidence le but poursuivi dans la Blades Residence, présentée ici. Depuis ses premiers projets, Morphosis attache beaucoup d'importance au processus qui, après une analyse introspective complexe, débouche sur la construction. Des maquettes élaborées jouent un rôle tout au long de cette recherche évolutive.

Morphosis, Blades Residence, Santa Barbara, California, 1992–96.

Morphosis, Blades Residence, Santa Barbara, Kalifornien, 1992–96.

Morphosis, Blades Residence, Santa Barbara, Californie, 1992–96.

Blades Residence

Santa Barbara, California, 1992–1996

The architect Thom Mayne described this house as follows: "A large exterior room has been created within which the house is situated. This room embraces an augmented natural landscape conveying a sense of sanctuary... Through the fusion of the exterior and interior worlds, the individual gradually becomes oriented... learns to keep balance..." The goal of the architect was to create spaces that "bleed into each other" without precisely defined limits. The main living spaces are contained in a 30 meter long, 5 meter wide rectangular box rising at its highest point to 4.5 meters. Unlike modernist structures, which tended to give the impression of simply sitting on their sites, this house burrows into the ground, accentuating the architect's effort to fuse interior and exterior. As was the case with the Teiger House, built by Mayne's former partner Michael Rotondi, the client here, Richard Blades, was inspired by the Crawford Residence, Montecito, California (1987–92), built by Morphosis before Mayne and Rotondi split apart.

Page 135: The angular volumes of the Blades Residence give the impression that it is emerging from the earth. In itself, this fact sets the house apart from the modernist tradition, which rarely engaged the landscape in such a way.
Pages 136–137: An image shows the continuity of interior and exterior spaces.

Seite 135: Die kantigen Formen des Hauses vermitteln den Eindruck von aus dem Boden gewachsenen geologischen Formationen. Dadurch setzt es sich von der üblichen modernen Architektur ab, die nur selten derart eng mit der Landschaft verknüpft ist.
Seite 136–137: Die Abbildung zeigt, wie Innen- und Außenräume ineinander übergehen.

Page 135: Les volumes anguleux de la Blades Residence donnent l'impression qu'elle émerge du sol. Cette caractéristique diffère radicalement de la tradition moderniste dans laquelle le paysage n'est que rarement intégré de cette façon.
Pages 136–137: Continuité des espaces intérieurs et extérieurs.

Der Architekt Thom Mayne sagte folgendes zu seinem Einfamilienhaus: »Ein großer Außenraum wurde um das Haus herum geschaffen. Er umfaßt eine angereicherte natürliche Landschaft, die ein Gefühl von Heiligtum vermittelt... Infolge der Fusion von Außen- und Innenwelt orientiert sich der Mensch allmählich, ... lernt, sein Gleichgewicht zu halten...« Der Architekt wollte Räume schaffen, die ohne klare Grenzen »ineinander übergehen«. Die Hauptwohnräume sind in einem 30 m langen und 5 m breiten rechteckigen Kastenbau untergebracht, der an seiner höchsten Stelle 4,5 m hoch ist. Im Gegensatz zu modernen Bauten, die häufig den Eindruck erwecken, als säßen sie einfach platt auf dem Erdboden, gräbt sich dieses Haus in die Erde ein und akzentuiert damit die Bemühungen des Architekten, Innen- und Außenraum als eine Einheit zu gestalten. Wie schon beim Teiger House, das Maynes ehemaliger Partner Michael Rotondi baute, hatte sich auch in diesem Fall der Bauherr des Hauses, Richard Blades, als ein Vorbild vom Crawford House in Montecito, Kalifornien (1987–92), inspirieren lassen; dieses hatte Morphosis entworfen und gebaut, bevor Mayne und Rotondi beruflich getrennte Wege gingen.

L'architecte Thom Mayne décrit cette maison de la façon suivante: «Une grande pièce extérieure a été créée qui contient la maison. Elle comprend un paysage naturel qui lui confère un sentiment de sanctuarisation... Par la fusion des univers de l'extérieur et de l'intérieur, l'individu perçoit peu à peu une influence ... apprend à conserver un équilibre...» L'objectif de l'architecte était de créer des espaces qui «coulent l'un dans l'autre» sans limites nettement définies. Les principaux espaces de vie sont contenus dans une boîte rectangulaire de 30 m de long par cinq de large et s'élevant jusqu'à 4,5 m de haut. À la différence des structures modernistes qui tendent à donner l'impression d'avoir été posées sur le sol, cette maison s'enfonce dans la terre, accentuant l'effort de l'architecte de fusionner l'intérieur et l'extérieur. Comme pour Teiger House, construite par l'ancien partenaire de Mayne, Michael Rotondi, Richard Blades, le client, avait été séduit par la Crawford Residence de Montecito, Californie (1987–92), construite par Morphosis avant la séparation des deux associés.

Page 138, pages 140–141: *There is an interplay of levels and volumes of the house that leads the architect to speak of rooms that "bleed" into each other.*
Page 139: *A working model emphasizes the rapport of the building with its site.*

Seite 138, Seite 140–141: *Das Wechselspiel von Ebenen und Volumen ließ den Architekten von Räumen sprechen, die »ineinanderübergehen«.*
Seite 139: *Ein Arbeitsmodell verdeutlicht den Bezug des Hauses zu seinem Baugrund.*

Page 138, pages 140–141: *Le jeux des niveaux et des volumes de la maison a amené l'architecte à parler de pièces qui «coulent» les unes dans les autres.*
Page 139: *Une maquette de travail met en évidence le rapport entre la construction et son site.*

Eric Owen Moss

The architect Philip Johnson has called Eric Owen Moss, born in Los Angeles in 1943, "a jeweler of junk." In his work built to date, Moss has placed an emphasis on unusual materials. Old chains, broken trusses, and other incongruous elements take their place in his buildings, much as they might participate in a modern sculpture. His career has been unusual in that almost all of his work has been concentrated in a single area of Los Angeles, the so-called Hayden Tract located in Culver City. Here, together with the developers Frederick and Laurie Samitaur Smith, he has built and renovated more than 30,000 square meters of office space, mainly for the recording and electronics industries. Combining elements of existing warehouses with the new structures he has created buildings with a memory, which sometimes even includes his own unrealized ideas for the same spaces.

Der Architekt Philip Johnson nannte den 1943 in Los Angeles geborenen Eric Owen Moss einen »jeweler of junk«, was man mit »Ramsch-Juwelier« übersetzen könnte. In seinen bisher fertiggestellten Bauten hat Moss ungewöhnliche Materialien eingesetzt. Alte Ketten, geborstene Träger und andere »unpassende« Schrott-Teile finden in diesen Gebäuden ihren Platz – ähnlich wie bei manchen modernen Skulpturen. Seine berufliche Laufbahn ist insofern ungewöhnlich, als er fast alle seine Bauten in einem einzigen Stadtareal von Los Angeles realisiert hat, dem sogenannten Hayden Tract in Culver City. Hier hat er für das Investorenehepaar Frederick und Laurie Samitaur Smith über 30 000 m² Büroflächen erstellt oder modernisiert, vor allem für Elektronikfirmen und Tonstudios. Indem er die alten Lagerhäuser mit Neubauten kombinierte, hat Moss »Gebäude mit Gedächtnis« geschaffen, die manchmal sogar an seine eigenen früheren Entwürfe für denselben Standort erinnern.

D'Eric Owen Moss (né en 1943), l'architecte Philip Johnson a écrit qu'il était «un orfèvre en ferraille». Dans son œuvre, ce jeune architecte californien a jusqu'à présent beaucoup joué avec des matériaux inhabituels. Vieilles chaînes, poutres brisées et autres éléments incongrus trouvent leur place dans ses réalisations, un peu comme dans une sculpture contemporaine. Sa carrière sort des schémas classiques dans la mesure où la quasi totalité de son œuvre se concentre dans un seul quartier de Los Angeles, le Hayden Tract, à Culver City. En compagnie des promoteurs Frederick et Laurie Samitaur Smith, il a construit et rénové plus de 30 000 m² de bureaux, principalement pour des sociétés d'électronique ou d'enregistrement. Associant des éléments d'entrepôts existants déjà à de nouvelles structures, il a créé des immeubles qui ont un passé, allant parfois jusqu'à inclure des projets non réalisés qu'il avait conçus pour le même espace.

Eric Owen Moss, Prittard & Sullivan Building, Culver City, California, 1995–97.

Eric Owen Moss, Prittard & Sullivan-Bau, Culver City, Kalifornien, 1995–97.

Eric Owen Moss, Prittard & Sullivan Building, Culver City, Californie, 1995–97.

Prittard & Sullivan Building

Culver City, California, 1995–1997

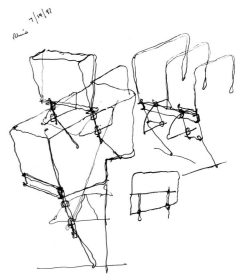

This corporate headquarters for a video and film computer graphics company is the most recent addition to the renovation of the so-called Hayden Tract in Culver City by Eric Owen Moss and the developers Frederick and Laurie Samitaur Smith. Measuring 5,000 square meters, the structure incorporates elements of a an pre-existing structure such as bowstring trusses. Going beyond his usual use of such recovered elements in a sculptural idiom, the architect also includes projected uses for the same space within the final design. A house he planned to build here at one point finds its ghostly presence integrated into the lobby, for example. With an exterior finishing of cement, plaster and glass, the Prittard & Sullivan Building is a rigid steel frame structure with wood and light gauge metal frame infill. Located midway between downtown Los Angeles and Santa Monica, Culver City, a largely rundown community is thus finding new life, thanks to Moss and the Smiths.

Dieses Hauptgebäude einer Video- und Filmfirma für Computerbildtechnik mit 5 000 m² Nutzfläche ist der neueste Zuwachs im sogenannten Hayden Tract in Culver City, das Eric Owen Moss zusammen mit den Bauinvestoren Frederick und Laurie Samitaur Smith realisiert hat. Dabei verwendete er Teile eines Altbaus, z.B. Zugbandträger, und zwar nicht nur im plastischen »Idiom« seiner früheren Bauten, sondern darüber hinaus auch unter dem Aspekt künftiger Nutzungsänderungen des schließlich ausgeführten Entwurfs. Die Form eines Hauses, das er früher einmal für dieses Grundstück geplant hatte, findet man z.B. in Gestalt des Eingangsfoyers wieder. Die Außenfassade ist aus Zement, Putz und Glas, das Tragwerk eine feste Stahlrahmenkonstruktion, ausgefacht mit Holz und schmalen Metallrahmenelementen. Culver City, einem ziemlich heruntergekommenen Ort auf halbem Weg zwischen der Downtown von Los Angeles und Santa Monica, wird so mit Hilfe von Moss und den Smiths wieder neues Leben eingehaucht.

Ce siège social d'une société de production de vidéo et de film en images de synthèse est le plus récent ajout à la rénovation du «Hayden Tract» à Culver City par Eric Owen Moss et les promoteurs Frederick et Laurie Samitaur Smith. Sur 5 000 m², la structure incorpore des éléments d'une construction préexistante, comme une charpente en arc. Dépassant son utilisation fréquente d'éléments récupérés au service de son langage sculptural, l'architecte a évoqué ici des utilisations possibles de l'espace. Par exemple, une maison qu'il voulait construire à un certain moment trouve son expression fantomatique dans le hall d'entrée. Avec des finitions extérieures en ciment, plâtre et verre, le Prittard & Sullivan Building est une structure à ossature d'acier complétée à l'intérieur par une structure en bois et métal léger. Situé à mi-chemin entre le centre de Los Angeles et Santa Monica, Culver City, quartier en grande partie abandonné, retrouve une nouvelle vie grâce à Moss et aux Smith.

Despite the simplicity of its basic floor plan, the Prittard & Sullivan Building incorporates numerous elements of the structure which existed previously on the same site, as well as the sculptural incursions of the architect.

Trotz der Einfachheit des Grundrisses umfaßt das Prittard & Sullivan Building zahlreiche Elemente des früher auf diesem Gelände stehenden Hauses sowie plastische »Zutaten« des Architekten.

Sous l'apparente simplicité de son plan, le Prittard & Sullivan Building incorpore de nombreux éléments d'une construction préexistante, ainsi que des incursions de l'architecte dans le domaine de la sculpture.

Eric Owen Moss: Prittard & Sullivan Building, 1995–97 **145**

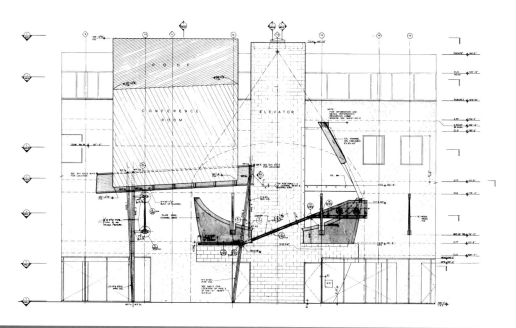

The computer drawings on page 147 give a particularly clear view of the structure of the building, of the interior circulation, and of the sculpted exterior volumes.

Die Computermodelle auf Seite 147 verdeutlichen sowohl die Konstruktion, die Innenverkehrsflächen als auch die plastische Ausformung des Gebäudes.

Le dessins à l'ordinateur page 147 donnent une vue particulièrement claire de la structure du bâtiment, des circulations intérieures et des volumes sculptés de l'extérieur.

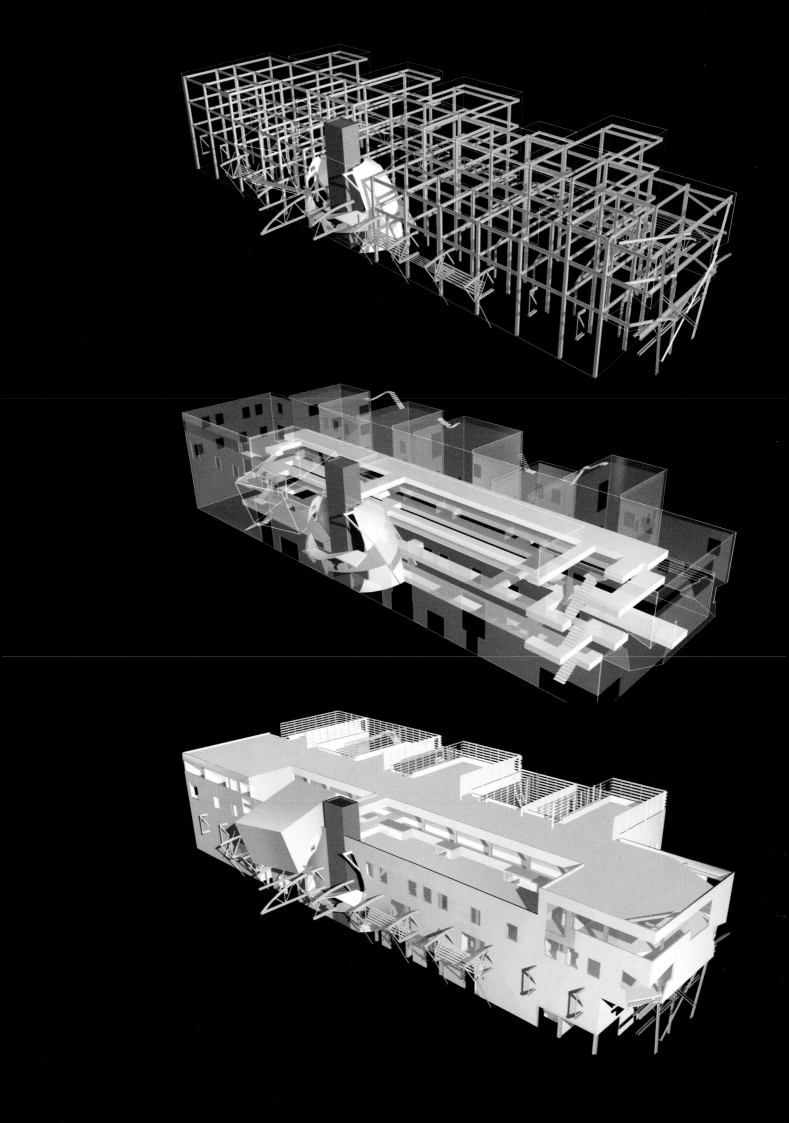

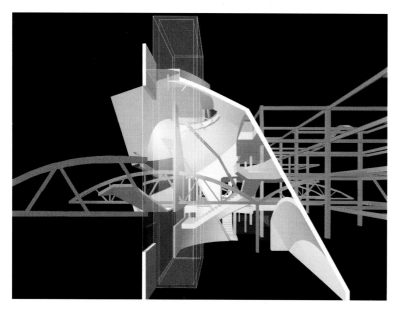

Recalling The Box, another Eric Owen Moss building located nearby, Prittard & Sullivan includes a tilted box-like element which appears to be tumbling out of place.

In Anlehnung an The Box, einem anderen Gebäude von Eric Owen Moss in Culver City, hat der Prittard & Sullivan-Bau einen geneigten Kastenteil, der aussieht, als würde er gleich abstürzen.

Rappelant The Box, autre réalisation d'Eric Owen Moss à proximité, le Prittard & Sullivan comprend également une sorte de boîte penchée qui semble prête à basculer.

As is typical of Eric Owen Moss's buildings, the volumetric complexity of this office does not interfere with its clarity and its usefulness as working space.

Charakteristisch für die Architektur von Moss ist die räumliche Komplexität, die auch bei diesem Bürobau keineswegs die Klarheit und Funktionalität der Arbeitsplätze stört.

Typique des réalisations d'Eric Owen Moss, la complexité volumétrique de cet immeuble de bureau n'interfère pas pour autant avec sa lisibilité et sa fonctionnalité.

Ieoh Ming Pei

Undoubtedly one of the best-known architects in the world, I.M. Pei built his reputation in good part with major museum projects such as the East Building of the National Gallery of Art in Washington D.C., located on the Mall near Capital Hill, or the Pyramid of the Louvre in Paris (Grand Louvre, 1983–93), which is the most visible part of his complete reorganization of the largest museum in France. Contested for political reasons at the outset, the Pyramid has since become one of the symbols of France, reproduced as often as the Eiffel Tower. Though strictly American architectural circles may not fully understand the significance of projects such as the Louvre or the Miho Museum in Japan, they do place I.M. Pei in a category apart, in the very restricted circle of the most significant architects of the latter half of the century. Born in 1917 in Canton, educated at Harvard, I.M. Pei continues to work on a number of large projects simultaneously, including towers in Beijing and Jakarta, and a museum of modern art in Luxembourg.

I.M. Pei ist zweifellos einer der weltweit bekanntesten Architekten. Sein Ruf gründet sich zu einem Gutteil auf große Museumsbauten wie das East Building der National Gallery of Art in Washington D.C., an der Mall in der Nähe des Capitol Hill, oder die Louvre-Pyramide in Paris (Grand Louvre, 1983–93), sichtbarster Teil einer umfassenden Umgestaltung des größten Museums in Frankreich. Aus politischen Gründen zunächst umstritten, ist die Pyramide seither zu einem Wahrzeichen Frankreichs aufgestiegen, ebenso häufig reproduziert wie der Eiffel-Turm. Obwohl I.M. Pei in der amerikanischen Architekturszene vielleicht nicht auf volles Verständnis stößt, wird er hier doch zu einem sehr kleinen Kreis der bedeutendsten amerikanischen Architekten in der zweiten Hälfte unseres Jahrhunderts gezählt. 1917 in Kanton geboren und in Harvard ausgebildet, arbeitet I.M. Pei auch weiterhin gleichzeitig an einer Reihe von Großprojekten, u.a. Hochhäusern in Peking und Jakarta und einem Museum für moderne Kunst in Luxemburg.

Certainement l'un des architectes les plus célèbres au monde, I.M. Pei a édifié une bonne partie de sa réputation sur de grands projets muséaux comme l'East Building de la National Gallery of Art de Washington, située sur le Mall près de Capitol Hill, ou la Pyramide du Louvre à Paris (Grand Louvre, 1983–93), l'élément le plus visible de la restructuration complète du plus grand musée français. Contestée au départ pour des raisons politiques, la Pyramide est devenue l'un des symboles de Paris, aussi souvent reproduite que la tour Eiffel. Bien que les cercles américains de spécialistes de l'architecture ne comprennent pas pleinement le sens des projets comme le Louvre ou le Musée Miho au Japon, ils n'en placent pas moins I.M. Pei dans une catégorie à part, celle des architectes les plus importants de la fin de ce siècle. Né en 1917 à Canton, formé à Harvard, I.M. Pei continue à travailler sur plusieurs grands projets simultanément, dont des tours à Pékin et à Djakarta et un musée d'art moderne à Luxembourg.

I.M. Pei, Miho Museum, Shigaraki, Shiga, Japan, 1992–97. The main entrance door.

I.M. Pei, Miho Museum, Shigaraki, Shiga, Japan, 1992–97. Der Haupteingang.

I.M. Pei, Musée Miho, Shigaraki, Shiga, Japon, 1992–97. La porte d'entrée principale.

Page 154: *A distant view shows just how pristine the natural environment around the building remains, located within a nature preserve.*
Page 155: *A sketch by I.M. Pei shows how the Miho Museum fits into its mountainous setting.*

Seite 154: *Eine Aufnahme aus der Ferne offenbart, wie unberührt die Landschaft um das Museumsgebäude geblieben ist.*
Seite 155: *Eine Skizze von I.M. Pei zeigt, wie das Miho Museum sich in seine Umgebung einfügt.*

Page 154: *Une vue de loin montre à quel point l'environnement naturel a été respecté.*
Page 155: *Esquisse de I.M. Pei montrant l'intégration du Musée Miho dans son cadre montagneux.*

Miho Museum
Shigaraki, Shiga, Japan, 1992–1997

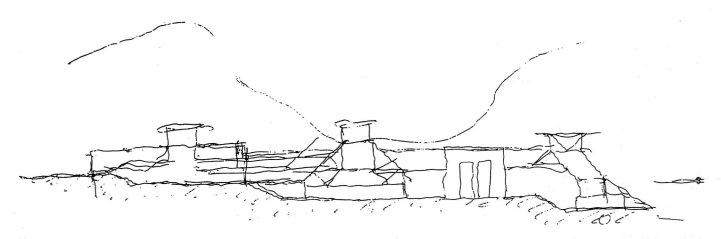

Located in the Shigaraki Mountains about one and a half hours by car from Kyoto, the Miho Museum is set in a nature reserve. The topography of the site and local environmental restrictions required that some 85% of the structure be underground. The museum is approached through a 200 meter long tunnel followed by an asymmetrical post-tensioned cable bridge measuring 120 meters in length. Only 1,830 square meters of the roof area, mainly in the form of skylights, are visible, while some 5,608 square meters are located beneath landscaped areas. The building is finished with Magny Doré limestone from France, for both the exterior walls and the interior, with Kulla Swedish granite for the entrance steps. The site itself measures no less than 1 million square meters, and the museum building has a gross building area of 17,429 square meters on three levels. Exhibition areas within include the South Wing (1,000 square meters) for non-Japanese antiquities, ranging from ancient Egypt to a major Persian carpet woven at the end of the 16th century; and the North Wing (also 1,000 square meters), which is used for the display of Japanese art. Built by the Osaka firm Shimizu, the Miho Museum is an exercise in the highest quality of design and construction.

Das Miho Museum steht etwa anderthalb Autostunden von Kyoto entfernt in einem Naturschutzgebiet in den Shigaraki-Bergen. Die Geländetopographie und lokale Umweltschutzauflagen machten es erforderlich, den Bau zu 85% unterirdisch anzulegen. Der Zugang zum Museum erfolgt über einen 200 m langen Tunnel, gefolgt von einer asymmetrischen, 120 m langen Spanndrahtbrücke. Nur 1830 m² der Dachfläche sind sichtbar, vor allem in Form von Dachlaternen, 5608 m² sind von Grünflächen bedeckt. Die Innen- und Außenwandverkleidungen bestehen aus französischem Magny-Doré-Kalkstein, die Eingangsstufen aus schwedischem Kulla-Granit. Das ganze Gelände umfaßt nicht weniger als eine Million Quadratmeter, und das Museum besitzt 17429 m² Gesamtfläche auf drei Ebenen. Ausstellungsbereiche sind im Südflügel (1000 m²) für die nicht-japanische Antikensammlung (von altägyptischen Objekten bis zu einem kostbaren persischen Teppich aus dem 16. Jh.) und im Nordflügel (ebenfalls 1000 m²) für japanische Kunst vorhanden. Das von dem in Osaka ansässigen Bauunternehmen Shimizu errichtete Miho Museum ist eine höchst stil- und qualitätvolle Entwurfs- und Konstruktionsarbeit. Obwohl der Gesamtplan im Laufe des Entwurfsprozesses

À environ une heure et demie de voiture de Kyoto, le Musée Miho se trouve en pleine nature protégée, dans les montagnes de la préfecture de Shigaraki. La topographie et la réglementation locale sur l'environnement ont fait que 85% de la construction sont enfouie sous terre. L'accès au musée passe par un tunnel de 200 m de long, suivi par un pont à haubans asymétrique de 120 m de long. Seuls 1830 m² de toits, essentiellement des verrières, sont visibles, tandis que 5608 m² sont en dessous des zones paysagées. Le bâtiment est recouvert de pierre bourguignonne dorée de Magny, à la fois à l'extérieur et à l'intérieur, les escaliers d'entrée étant en granit suédois de Kulla. Le terrain lui-même ne mesure pas moins d'un million de m², et le bâtiment du musée compte 17429 m² répartis sur trois niveaux. Les surfaces d'exposition intérieures comprennent l'aile sud (1000 m²) pour les antiquités non japonaises – des objets de l'Égypte ancienne jusqu'à un important tapis persan de la fin du XVIᵉ siècle – et l'aile nord (1000 m² également) consacrée à la présentation des collections d'art japonais. Construit par l'entreprise d'Osaka Shimizu, le musée de Miho est un exercice de conception et de construction de la plus haute qualité. Bien que le plan de masse ait été modifié, et que des

Despite the fact that the overall plan changed in the course of design work, and that structural changes were made even after construction had begun, the museum gives an impression of great harmony and peace. A bell tower built by I.M. Pei for the same group some two kilometers away is visible through many of the museum's windows, accentuating his presence in this beautiful natural site. Working with such fine collaborators as Chris Rand and Tim Culbert, who succeeded each other in the role of Architect-in-Charge, I.M. Pei has proven once again that he is able to master exceedingly complex architectural situations in a masterful way. Calling on his extensive knowledge of architectural history, Pei has succeeded in calling on the tradition of Japanese temple architecture in this building, while remaining entirely modern.

Änderungen erfuhr und nach Baubeginn auch das Tragwerk noch revidiert wurde, vermittelt der Bau ruhige Harmonie und Geschlossenheit. Viele Fenster des Museums bieten Ausblick auf einen Glockenturm, den I.M. Pei für die Shûmeikai in etwa 2 km Entfernung in dieser landschaftlich wunderschönen Umgebung baute. I.M. Pei hatte für dieses Bauvorhaben in Chris Rand und Tim Culbert nacheinander kompetente Projektleiter, die ihm zu beweisen halfen, daß er in der Lage ist, außerordentlich komplexe architektonische Aufgaben meisterhaft zu erfüllen. Indem er aus dem reichen Fundus seiner bauhistorischen Kenntnisse schöpfte, ist es Pei gelungen, mit diesem Museumsgebäude an japanische Tempelarchitektur zu erinnern und trotzdem ganz modern zu bauen.

changements structurels aient été apportés pendant le chantier, le musée donne une impression de paix et de grande harmonie. Un campanile, élevé par I.M. Pei pour le même organisme à 2 km environ, s'aperçoit à travers de nombreuses baies du musée, ce qui accentue son impact visuel dans ce magnifique site naturel. Grâce également à des collaborateurs de qualité, comme Chris Rand et Tim Culbert, qui se sont succédés comme architecte de chantier, I.M. Pei a prouvé une fois encore qu'il sait maîtriser des problèmes architecturaux excessivement complexes. En s'appuyant sur sa connaissance approfondie de l'histoire de l'architecture, il a réussi à évoquer la tradition des temples japonais tout en restant résolument moderne.

Page 156: *A view of the entrance pavilion.*
Page 157: *Taken from above the arc of the bridge, this picture shows the museum entrance, and in the distance the roof of the sanctuary of Shinji-Shûmeikai by Minoru Yamasaki, and, to the left, Pei's Bell Tower for the same group.*

Seite 156: *Ansicht des Eingangspavillons.*
Seite 157: *Die Aufnahme von oberhalb des Brückenbogens zeigt den Museumseingang und in der Ferne das Dach des Shinji-Shûmeikai Tempels von Minoru Yamasaki. Links im Bild I.M. Peis Glockenturm für die gleiche Baugruppe.*

Page 156: *Vue du pavillon d'entrée.*
Page 157: *Vue prise en plongée de l'arc du pont montrant l'entrée du musée et, dans le lointain, le toit du sanctuaire de Shinji-Shûmeikai par Minoru Yamasaki, et, à gauche, le clocher construit par Pei pour la même organisation.*

RECEPTION PAVILLION

Page 158: *An overall site plan (top) shows the entrance pavilion, bridge, tunnel and museum. Below, a detail of the tunnel lighting.*
Pages 158–159: *Looking back into the tunnel, an image taken from the deck of the bridge.*

Seite 158: *Der Geländeplan (oben) zeigt die Lage von Eingangspavillon, Brücke, Tunnel und Museums-gebäude. Darunter ein Detail der Tunnelbeleuchtung.*
Seite 158–159: *Blick zurück in den Tunnel.*
Das Foto wurde von der Brücke aus aufgenommen.

Page 158: *Plan général du site (en haut) montrant le pavillon d'entrée, le pont, le tunnel et le musée.*
Ci-dessus, détail de l'éclairage du tunnel.
Pages 158–159: *Vue prise du tablier du pont, vers le tunnel.*

Pages 160–161: As is typical of Pei, the 120 meter asymmetrical post-tensioned cable bridge, designed by I.M. Pei Architect and Leslie E. Robertson Associates, structural engineers, is a work of elegant perfection, at once modern and respectful of its natural setting.
Pages 162–163: An image of the roof of the museum, which is 85% underground.

Seite 160–161: Die 120 m lange, asymmetrische Spanndrahtbrücke (Entwurf: I.M. Pei mit Tragwerksplanern Leslie E. Robertson Associates) ist – typisch Pei – ein Werk eleganter Perfektion, modern und zugleich voller Respekt für ihren landschaftlichen Standort.
Seite 162–163: Blick über die Dachlandschaft des Museums, das zu 85% in die Erde eingegraben ist.

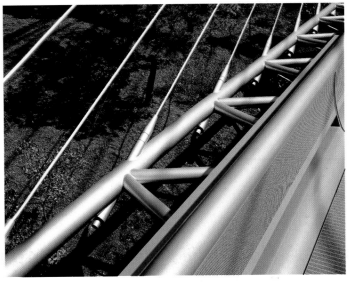

Pages 160–161: Comme il est typique chez Pei, le pont à haubans asymétrique de 120 m de long, conçu en collaboration avec Leslie E. Robertson Associates, ingénieurs de construction, est une œuvre d'une élégante perfection, à la fois moderne et respectueuse de son environnement naturel.
Pages 162–163: Vue du toit du musée qui est souterrain à 85%.

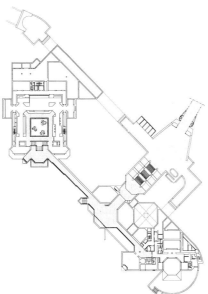

Pages 164–165: The main entrance.
Page 165: A plan of the entrance level. Below, two images show the rapport between exterior and interior.
Pages 166–167: A view of the main entrance area.

Seite 164–165: Ansicht des Haupteinganges.
Seite 165: Grundriß des Erdgeschosses. Darunter zwei Aufnahmen, die die Beziehung von Außen- und Innenraum veranschaulichen.
Seite 166–167: Innenansicht des Eingangspavillons.

Pages 164–165: L'entrée principale.
Page 165: Plan du niveau de l'entrée, ci-dessous deux photographies qui illustrent les rapports entre l'extérieur et l'intérieur.
Pages 166–167: Vue de la zone de l'entrée principale.

Pages 168–169: *To the left, a view of the Japanese garden in the North Wing. Below, two images of works of art in the South Wing. The structure was specially modified to house the 5.94 meter long "Medallion and Animal Carpet."*

Seite 168–169: *Der japanische Garten des Nordflügels (links)und zwei Innenansichten des Südflügels mit Kunstwerken. Die Konstruktion wurde speziell abgeändert, damit der 5,94 m lange Medaillon-Teppich gehängt werden konnte.*

Pages 168–169: *Vue du jardin japonais de l'aile nord (à gauche). Ci-dessous, deux images des œuvres d'art exposées dans l'aile sud. Le bâtiment a été modifié pour accueillir le tapis de 5,94 m de long, nommé «Le médaillon et l'animal».*

RoTo

Clark Stevens

Michael Rotondi

Michael Rotondi was a partner of Thom Mayne in the firm Morphosis from 1980 to 1991. He has been the director of SCI-Arc since 1987. Clark Stevens and Michael Rotondi created RoTo Architects in 1991. Although their approach remains as intensely intellectual as that of Morphosis, they have evolved toward the idea that an architect should not maintain "singular control" over the design process. Clients and others are called to give their opinions during an open-ended interaction. As Rotondi says, "The search is for a zone, an in-between state, the confusion in the transformation from one state of rest to another, where neither dominates. The third state can still have evidence of the original two." Or again, "In nature, complex systems are layered interdependently to compose essential beauty." The projects of RoTo include CDLT 1,2 (Silverlake, Califorina, 1991), the Nicola Restaurant (Los Angeles, California, 1992–93), and the Carlson-Reges Residence (Los Angeles, California, 1993–96), as well as the Teiger House published here.

Michael Rotondi war der Partner von Thom Mayne im Architekturbüro Morphosis von 1980 bis 1991. Seit 1987 ist er Direktor des Southern California Institute of Architecture (SCI-Arc). Zusammen mit seinem Kollegen Clark Stevens gründete er 1991 das Büro RoTo Architects. Obwohl ihr Ansatz ebenso intellektuell geblieben ist wie der von Morphosis, meinen sie, daß ein Architekt nicht die »alleinige Kontrolle« über den Entwurfsprozeß ausüben sollte. Bauherren und andere werden in einer zeitlich nicht begrenzten Diskussion um ihre Meinung zum Entwurf befragt. Rotondi sagt: »Wir suchen nach einem Zwischenzustand der Konfusion, einer Übergangszone der Veränderung von einem Ruhezustand zum anderen, in dem keiner von beiden dominiert. Der dritte Zustand kann immer noch Spuren der beiden ursprünglichen Zustände aufweisen.« Er fährt fort: »In der Natur überlagern sich voneinander abhängige komplexe Systeme und komponieren auf diese Weise vollkommene Schönheit.« Wichtige Projekte von RoTo Architects sind CDLT 1,2 (Silverlake, California, 1991), das Nicola Restaurant (Los Angeles, California, 1992–93), die Carlson-Reges Residence (Los Angeles, California, 1993–96) sowie das hier publizierte Teiger House.

Michael Rotondi a été associé avec Thom Mayne dans l'agence Morphosis de 1980 à 1991. Il dirige SCI-Arc depuis 1987. Clark Stevens et Michael Rotondi ont créé RoTo Architects en 1991. Bien que leur approche demeure aussi intellectuelle que celle de Mayne, elle a évolué vers l'idée que l'architecte ne devait pas maintenir son «contrôle singulier» sur le processus de conception. Les clients, entre autres, sont invités à exprimer leur opinion dans un processus interactif non limité dans le temps. Rotondi précise: «Il s'agit de la recherche d'une zone, d'un espace intermédiaire, d'une confusion dans le passage d'un état arrêté à un autre, où ni le premier ni le second ne domine. Le troisième état peut encore porter en lui la trace des deux précédents... Dans la nature, les systèmes complexes se superposent en interdépendance pour accéder à une beauté qui relève de l'essence.» Les réalisation de RoTo comprennent CLDT 1,2 (Silverlake, Californie, 1991), le Nicola Restaurant (Los Angeles, Californie, 1992–93), la Carlson-Reges Residence (Los Angeles, Californie, 1993–96) et la Teiger House publiée dans ses pages.

RoTo, Teiger House, Somerset County, New Jersey, 1990–95.

Teiger House

Somerset County, New Jersey, 1990–1995

This 600 square meter house is located in a very beautiful residential area of New Jersey. It is situated on a knoll at the juncture between a forest and field, with views extending for almost 50 kilometers onto the neighboring countryside. RoTo, the firm created by Michael Rotondi and his partner Clark Stevens when he left Morphosis in 1991, was chosen by the client over twenty other firms. David Teiger gave the architects a twenty-five page brief to outline his requirements, and the project evolved in a complex pattern related to these needs, as well as the presence of the site, which is integrated into the house through such elements as the rough-hewn fieldstone found locally. A private wing with the master bedroom above, and a guest bedroom below, is oriented in an east-west direction, while a media room and guest suite in a separate pavilion are sited on a north-south axis. A kitchen, living room, and dining room are placed at the intersection of these two axes, with a gallery and library above.

Dieses Einfamilienhaus (600 m²) steht in einer landschaftlich sehr schönen Wohngegend von New Jersey auf einer Hügelkuppe an der Grenze zwischen Wald und Feld. Von dort kann man bis zu 50 km weit die Landschaft überblicken. RoTo, das 1991 nach der Trennung von Mayne (Morphosis) von Michael Rotondi mit Clark Stevens gegründete Büro, erhielt von 20 Bewerbern um diesen Auftrag den Zuschlag. David Teigers 25-seitiger Anforderungskatalog gab die Grundlage für die komplexe Raumgliederung zur Erfüllung aller Bauherrenwünsche, und auch das Grundstück war mitbestimmend für den Entwurf, was etwa an den verwendeten grob behauenen Feldsteinen ersichtlich ist. Ein Privatwohnflügel mit Elternschlafzimmer im Obergeschoß und einem Gästezimmer im Erdgeschoß steht auf der Ost-West-Achse, ein »Medienraum« und Gästeappartement auf der Nord-Süd-Achse. Küche, Wohnraum und Eßzimmer, mit Galerie und Bibliothek auf der oberen Ebene, bilden die Schnittstelle dieser beiden Achsen.

Cette maison de 600 m² est située dans une magnifique zone résidentielle du New Jersey, sur un tertre à la limite de la forêt et des champs. La vue sur la campagne porte à près de 50 km à la ronde. RoTo, l'agence fondée par Michael Rotondi et son associé Clark Stevens lors de son départ de Morphosis en 1991, a été choisie par le client parmi 20 autres propositions. David Teiger a remis aux architectes un briefing de 25 pages, et le projet a évolué de manière complexe en fonction de ses besoins, et en tenant compte de la forte présence du site, qui se retrouve dans la maison même à travers divers éléments, comme la pierre locale grossièrement équarrie. L'aile privée contenant la chambre du propriétaire de la maison à l'étage et une chambre d'amis en dessous est orientée est-ouest, tandis qu'une pièce pour les médias et une suite pour les invités se trouvent dans un pavillon séparé, orienté sur un axe nord-sud. La cuisine, la salle-de-séjour et la salle-à-manger sont disposées à l'intersection de ces deux axes, et surmontées d'une galerie et d'une bibliothèque.

Page 172: The Teiger House is closely related to its beautiful natural setting.
Page 173: An aerial view shows the swimming pool perpendicular to the main volume of the house.

Seite 172: Das Teiger House ist eng mit seiner wunderschönen Umgebung verbunden.
Seite 173: Eine Luftaufnahme zeigt das Schwimmbecken im rechten Winkel zum Hauptbaukörper des Hauses.

Page 172: La Teiger House est étroitement intégrée à son superbe cadre naturel.
Page 173: La vue aérienne montre la piscine perpendiculaire au volume principal de la maison.

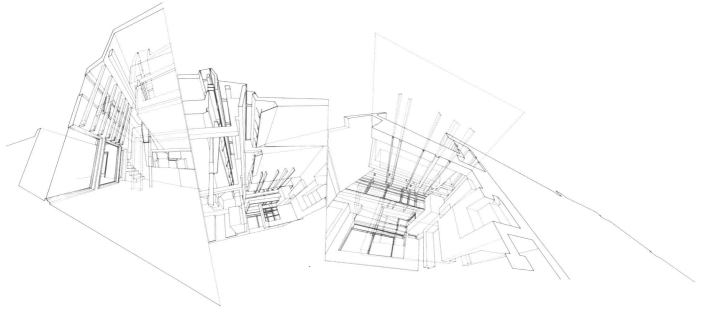

Despite the apparently geometric nature of some of the forms, the Teiger House is quite specifically not a modernist structure. Its complexity and its relation to the natural setting distance it from that tradition. To the right, a space for the owner's collection of folk art.

Trotz der offenbar geometrischen Formen ist das Teiger House eben doch kein Bauwerk der klassischen Moderne. Seine Vielgestaltigkeit und sein Eingehen auf die natürliche Umgebung distanziert es von dieser Tradition. Rechts ein Raum für die Volkskunstsammlung des Bauherrn.

Malgré la nature apparemment géométrique de ses formes, la Teiger House n'est pas pour autant une construction moderniste. Sa complexité et sa relation avec son cadre naturel la placent à part de cette tradition. À droite, un espace réservé à la collection d'art populaire du propriétaire.

Cantilevered volumes, stone from the site for the fire-place, and a sense of spatial complexity are immediate-ly evident in these photographs of the living room and kitchen, which open out into each other.

Vorkragende Geschoßteile, Natursteine aus der Region an der Kaminwand und räumliche Vielfalt sind die hervorstechenden Merkmale der Innenräume, die ineinander übergehen.

Des volumes en porte-à-faux et une cheminée en pierre trouvée sur le terrain créent une complexité spatiale très forte, comme le montrent ces deux vues de la salle-de-séjour et de la cuisine qui s'interpénètrent.

Thompson and Rose

Born in 1960, Maryann Thompson received her B.A. degree in Architecture at Princeton, and Masters degrees in Landscape Architecture and Architecture from Harvard. Her husband and partner, Charles Rose, born in 1960, also attended Princeton, and obtained his Master of Architecture from Harvard. They obtained their first commission while still students in 1987 for the Hartsbrook School, located in Hadley, Massachusetts. In this project, as in subsequent ones, such as the Atlantic Arts Center published here, they have made an effort to integrate landscape and architecture into a coherent whole. Influenced by travel to Kyoto and Suzhou, China, in 1983, they cite Michael Graves, Rafael Moneo, Denise Scott Brown, and the landscape architect Michael Van Valkenburgh as being amongst those who have had an impact on their work. Their recently completed Bartholomew County Veteran's Memorial (Columbus, Indiana), consisting of twenty-five 12 meter tall lime-stone pillars arranged in a square grid, has been extensively covered. In 1996, they have also worked with David Teiger (RoTo's client for the Teiger House published in this volume) on two projects, a 3,000 square meter office for Gemini Consulting (Cambridge, Massachusetts), and an office for "an independent film producer" in Bedminster, New Jersey.

Maryann Thompson wurde 1960 geboren, studierte Architektur in Princeton (B.A.) und Landschaftsarchitektur und Architektur in Harvard (M. Arch.). Ihr Ehemann und Büropartner Charles Rose (geb. 1960) studierte ebenfalls in Princeton und schloß sein Studium in Harvard mit einem M. Arch. ab. Ihren ersten Auftrag erhielten sie 1987, als sie noch Studenten waren, und zwar zum Bau der Hartsbrook School in Hadley, Massachusetts. Bei diesem Schulgebäude und bei folgenden Bauten, z.B. dem hier vorgestellten Atlantic Arts Center haben sie sich bemüht, Landschaft und Architektur zu einem Ganzen zu verbinden. Beeinflußt von Reisen nach Japan (Kyoto) und China (Sutschou) im Jahr 1983, führen sie als einflußgebend darüber hinaus Michael Graves, Rafael Moneo, Denise Scott Brown und den Landschaftsarchitekten Michael Van Valkenburgh an. Ihr kürzlich vollendetes Bartholomew County Veteran's Memorial (Columbus, Indiana) aus 25 12 m hohen Kalksteinsäulen auf quadratischem Rasterplan ist vielfach publiziert worden. 1996 haben sie auch für David Teiger (RoTos Bauherrn für das Teiger House) zwei Projekte bearbeitet, ein Bürohaus mit 3000 m² Fläche für Gemini Consulting, Cambridge, Massachusetts, und ein Büro für »einen unabhängigen Filmproduzenten« in Bedminster, New Jersey.

Née en 1960, Maryann Thompson a passé son B.A. en architecture à Princeton, et ses M.A. en architecture du paysage et architecture à Harvard. Son mari et associé, Charles Rose, né en 1960, a suivi la même filière. Encore étudiants, ils reçoivent leur première commande en 1987, la Hartsbrook School, à Hadley, Massachusetts. Dans ce projet, comme dans les suivants, dont l'Atlantic Arts Center reproduit ici, ils s'efforcent d'intégrer l'architecture et le paysage en un tout cohérent. Influencés par des voyages à Kyoto et à Suzhou, Chine, en 1983, ils citent Michael Graves, Rafael Moneo, Denise Scott Brown et l'architecte paysager Michael Van Valkenburgh parmi leurs influences. Ils ont récemment achevé le Mémorial des vétérans du comté de Bartholomew (Columbus, Indiana) qui consiste en 25 piliers de pierre 12 m de haut disposés selon une grille carrée, et qui a fait l'objet de nombreux articles de presse. En 1996, ils ont également travaillé avec David Teiger (le client de RoTo pour Teiger House, également reproduite dans ce volume) sur deux projets, 3000 m² de bureaux pour Gemini Consulting (Cambridge, Massachusetts) et les bureaux d'un producteur de films indépendant à Bedminster, New Jersey.

Thompson and Rose, Atlantic Center for the Arts, New Smyrna Beach, Florida, 1994–97.

Thompson and Rose, Atlantic Center for the Arts, New Smyrna Beach, Florida, 1994–97.

Thompson and Rose, Atlantic Center for the Arts, New Smyrna Beach, Floride, 1994–97.

Atlantic Center for the Arts

New Smyrna Beach, Florida, 1994–1997

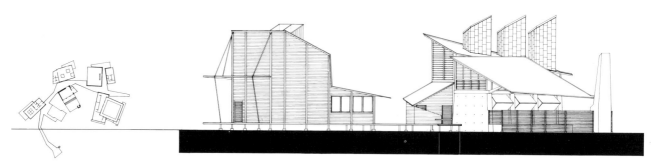

Built in a 30 hectare site, covered with dense jungle-like growth of palmetto shrubs, this group of six small buildings has been compared by its architects to a "conceptual work of art," or to the imperial villa of Katsura in Japan. Joined by a complex boardwalk, the buildings are intended as simple volumes for each of the disciplines covered by this arts center – theater, dance, sculpture, painting and music. The architects liken each of the spaces to clearings in the jungle. The shape of the buildings evolved not only as a result of the artistic disciplines but also in relation to budgetary and environmental considerations. The unusual roof forms, for example, had to be specially reinforced against potential hurricane-force winds. A sun-angle calculator was used to position each structure in an appropriate manner. A black-box theater was built, beginning in September 1994, and a second phase of construction began in March 1996. The project was completed in February 1997.

Die Architekten haben dieses Ensemble aus sechs kleinen Gebäuden auf einem 30 ha großen, dicht mit Palmen bewachsenen Gelände mit einem »konzeptuellen Kunstwerk« verglichen oder mit dem kaiserlichen Katsura-Palast in Japan. Ein einfacher Holzplankenweg verbindet die schlichten Gebäude miteinander. Sie sind jeweils für eine der hier geübten Disziplinen vorgesehen – Theater, Tanz, Bildhauerei, Malerei, Musik – und formal nicht nur Ausdruck dieser Künste, sondern auch Ergebnis finanzieller und ökologischer Überlegungen. Die ungewöhnlichen Dachformen mußten zusätzlich gegen potentielle Winde von Orkanstärke ausgesteift werden. Die Ausrichtung eines jeden Baus erfolgte mit Hilfe eines Sonnenwinkelmessers. Ab September 1994 entstand ein »black box«-Theater, die zweite Bauphase begann im März 1996. Das gesamte Center wurde im Februar 1997 fertiggestellt.

Édifié sur un terrain de 30 hectares, recouvert d'une végétation de palmiers, ce groupe de six petits bâtiments a été comparé par ses architectes à une «œuvre d'art conceptuelle», ou à la villa impériale de Katsura, au Japon. Reliées par un jeu complexe de cheminements de planches, les constructions se veulent de simples volumes consacrés à chacune des disciplines couvertes par ce centre artistique: théâtre, danse, sculpture, peinture et musique. Les architectes comparent chacun des ces espaces à une clairière dans la jungle. La forme de ces constructions a évolué pour des raisons programmatiques, mais aussi à cause des contraintes budgétaires et des considérations environnementales. Il a fallu, par exemple, renforcer les toits de forme curieuse pour résister aux tornades de la région. Un calculateur d'angles a permis de positionner chaque structure en fonction du soleil. Un théâtre a été construit en septembre 1994, et la seconde phase de construction a démarré en mars 1996. Le projet s'est achevé en février 1997.

The buildings are set along a boardwalk in the dense, jungle-like vegetation, with each designed to accommodate a specific form of artistic expression.

Die einzelnen Häuser sind an einem Holzplankenweg aufgereiht und umgeben von dichtem Dschungel. Jedes Haus dient einer bestimmten Form des künstlerischen Ausdrucks.

Les bâtiments sont disposés le long d'un passage en planches au milieu d'une végétation dense, chacun étant conçu pour accueillir une forme spécifique d'expression artistique.

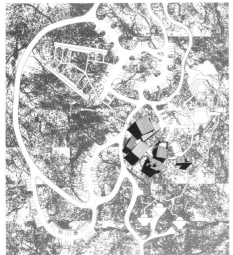

Pages 182–185: Unusual roof forms were designed to resist potential hurricane-force winds. The open, airy workspaces are intended as a refuge from and a contrast to the density of the natural environment.

Seite 182–185: *Die ungewöhnlichen Dachformen entstanden unter Berücksichtigung eventuell auftretender Sturmwinde. Die offenen, luftig hohen Arbeitsräume sollen Zufluchtstätte sein und sich zugleich von der dichten Vegetation absetzen.*

Pages 182–185: *Les toits de forme inhabituelle ont été dessinés pour résister aux tornades fréquentes dans la région. Les espaces de travail ouverts et aérés sont conçus comme des refuges au milieu d'un environnement naturel qui fait penser à une jungle.*

Biographies | Biographien

Center for Maximum Potential Building Systems
8604 F.M. 969
Austin, Texas 78724

Tel: + 1 512 928 4786
Fax: + 1 512 926 4418

Steven Ehrlich Architects
10865 Washington Boulevard
Culver City, California 90232

Tel : + 1 310 838 9700
Fax : + 1 310 838 9737

Frank O. Gehry & Associates, Inc.
1520-B Cloverfield Boulevard
Santa Monica, California 90404

Tel: + 1 310 828 6088
Fax: + 1 310 828 2098

CMPBS

Pliny Fisk III, born in New York in 1944, Co-Director of the Center for Maximum Potential Building Systems, received his B.A. from the University of Pennsylvania in 1967, a Masters in Architecture (1970) and a Masters in Landscape Architecture with an emphasis on Ecological Land Planning (1971) also from the University of Pennsylvania. His partner Gail Vittori, born in Washington, D.C. in 1954, attended the University of Massachusetts (1972–75). She is a specialist in sustainable design and waste management. They and their staff have worked on numerous master plans, such as that for the Armand Bayou Nature Center, Houston, Texas (1992–93); low income housing, Thelma, Texas (1994–95); Conservation Ledge Foundation, Matagorda Island, Texas (1996); the "Blueprint" Farm, Laredo, Texas (1988–90); and the Center for Wetland Studies, Baja del Sur, Mexico (1996–97). They have also acted as consultants to firms such as Apple Computer, Cupertino, California (1993–94).

Pliny Fisk III., Co-Direktor des CMPBS, wurde 1944 in New York geboren, machte seinen B.A. (1967), ein Masters-Diplom in Architektur (1970) und ein Masters-Diplom in Landschaftsarchitektur mit Schwerpunkt ökologische Landschaftspflege und Raumplanung (1971) an der University of Pennsylvania. Seine Partnerin Gail Vittori wurde 1954 in Washington D.C. geboren und besuchte die University of Massachusetts (1972–75). Sie ist Expertin für wiederverwertbares Design und Abfallversorgung/-verwertung. Fisk und Vittori sowie ihr Team haben an zahlreichen Musterplänen mitgewirkt, u.a.: Armand Bayou Nature Center, Houston, Texas (1992–93); Wohnsiedlung für Niedrigverdiener, Thelma, Texas (1994–95); Conservation Ledge Foundation, Matagorda Island, Texas (1996); »Blueprint« Farm, Laredo, Texas (1988–90) und das Center for Wetland Studies in Baja del Sur, Mexiko (1996–97). Außerdem sind sie als beratende Architekten tätig, u.a. für Apple Computer in Cupertino, Kalifornien (1993–94).

Né à New York en 1944, Pliny Fisk III est co-directeur du Center for Maximum Potential Building Systems. Études à l'Université de Pennsylvanie: B.A. en 1967, M.A. en architecture en 1970, et M.A. en architecture du paysage axé sur la programmation écologique des sols en 1971. Son associée, Gail Vittori, née à Washington D.C. en 1954, a étudié à l'Université du Massachusetts (1972–75). Elle est spécialisée dans le design recyclable et la gestion des déchets. Ils ont collaboré à de nombreux plans directeurs, dont celui de l'Armand Bayou Nature Center, Houston, Texas (1992–93); à des immeubles à loyers modérés, Thelma, Texas (1994–95); la Conservation Ledge Foundation de Matagorda Island, Texas (1996); la ferme «Blueprint», Laredo, Texas (1988–90)et le Center for Wetland Studies, Baja del Sur, Mexique (1996–97). Ils ont également travaillé comme consultants auprès d'entreprises comme Apple Computer, Cupertino, Californie (1993–94).

Steven Ehrlich

Born in New York in 1946, Steven Ehrlich received his B. Arch. degree from the Rensselaer Polytechnic Institute, Troy, New York in 1969. He studied indigenous vernacular architecture in North and West Africa from 1969 to 1977. He has completed numerous private residences, including the Friedman Residence (1986), the Ehrman-Coombs Residence in Santa Monica (1989–91), and the Schulman Residence in Brentwood (1989–92) – all in the Los Angeles area. Other built work includes the Shatto Recreation Center, Los Angeles (1991); Sony Music Entertainment Campus, Santa Monica (1993); Child Care Center for Sony, Culver City (1992–95); Game Show Network, Culver City (1995) as well as the Robertson Branch Library in Los Angeles (1993–97) – all in California. In 1997 his firm won three national AIA design awards.

Steven Ehrlich, 1946 in New York geboren, studierte Architektur am Rensselaer Polytechnic Institute in Troy, New York (B. Arch. 1969). Von 1969 bis 1977 erforschte er traditionelle Stammesarchitekturen in Nord- und Westafrika. Er hat zahlreiche Einfamilienhäuser gebaut, u.a. für die Friedmans (1986), die Familie Ehrman-Coombs in Santa Monica (1989–91) und die Schulmans in Brentwood (1989–92) – alle in der Gegend von Los Angeles. Wichtige Bauten: Shatto Recreation Center, Los Angeles (1991); Sony Music Entertainment Campus, Santa Monica (1993); Child Care Center für Sony in Culver City (1992–95); das Game Show Network in Culver City (1995) sowie die hier beschriebene Robertson Branch Library in Los Angeles (1993–97) – alle in Kalifornien. 1997 gewann seine Firma drei nationale AIA Design-Awards.

Né à New York en 1946, Steven Ehrlich passe son diplôme d'architecte au Rensselaer Polytechnic Institute, Troy, New York (B.A. 1969), avant d'étudier l'architecture vernaculaire de l'Afrique du Nord et de l'Ouest de 1969 à 1977. Il a réalisé de nombreuses résidences privées, dont la Friedman Residence (1986), la Ehrman-Coombs Residence, Santa Monica (1989–91), et la Schulman Residence, Brentwood (1989–92), toutes situées dans la région de Los Angeles. Il a également édifié le Shatto Recreation Center, Los Angeles (1991); le Sony Music Entertainment Campus, Santa Monica (1993); le Game Show Network, Culver City (1995); un Child Care Center, toujours pour Sony, Culver City (1992–95), et la Robertson Branch Library, Los Angeles (1993–97) – tous situés en Californie. En 1997, son entreprise remporta trois prix nationaux de l'AIA.

Frank O. Gehry

Born in Toronto, Canada in 1929, Frank O. Gehry studied at the University of Southern California, Los Angeles (1949–51) and at Harvard (1956–57). Principal of Frank O. Gehry & Associates, Inc., Los Angeles, since 1962, he received the 1989 Pritzker Prize. Some of his notable projects are the Loyola Law School, Los Angeles, California (1981–84); the Norton Residence, Venice, California (1983); California Aerospace Museum, Los Angeles, California (1982–84); Schnabel Residence, Brentwood, California (1989); Festival Disney, Marne-la-Vallée, France (1989–92); University of Toledo Art Building, Toledo, Ohio (1990–92); American Center, Paris, France (1993); Walt Disney Concert Hall, Los Angeles, California (1987–2001); Nationale Nederlanden Building, Rasin Embankment, Prague, Czech Republic (1992–96); and the Guggenheim Museum Bilbao, Bilbao, Spain (1991–97).

1929 in Toronto, Kanada, geboren, studierte Frank O. Gehry an der University of Southern California in Los Angeles (1949–51) und in Harvard (1956–57). Seit 1962 hat er sein eigenes Büro, Frank O. Gehry & Associates, Inc., in Los Angeles. 1989 erhielt er den Pritzker Prize. Zu seinen wichtigsten Bauten gehören: Loyola Law School, Los Angeles, Kalifornien (1981–84); Norton Residence, Venice, Kalifornien (1983); California Aerospace Museum in Los Angeles, Kalifornien (1982–84); Schnabel Residence, Brentwood, Kalifornien (1989); Festival Disney, Marne-la-Vallée, Frankreich (1989–92); University of Toledo Art Building, Toledo, Ohio (1990–92); American Center in Paris, Frankreich (1993); Walt Disney Concert Hall, Los Angeles, Kalifornien (1987–2001); Nationale Nederlanden Building, Prag, Republik Tschechien (1992–96) und das Guggenheim Museum Bilbao, Bilbao, Spanien (1991–97).

Né à Toronto, Canada en 1929. Études: University of Southern California, Los Angeles (1949–51) et Harvard (1956–57). Responsable de Frank O. Gehry & Associates, Inc., Los Angeles, Californie, depuis 1962. Pritzker Prize en 1989. Parmi ses principales réalisations: Loyola Law School, Los Angeles, Californie (1981–84); Norton Residence, Venice, Californie (1983); California Aerospace Museum, Los Angeles, Californie (1982–84); Schnabel Residence, Brentwood, Californie (1989); Festival Disney, Marne-La-Vallée, France (1989–92); University of Toledo Art Building, Toledo, Ohio (1990–92); American Center, Paris, France (1993); Walt Disney Concert Hall, Los Angeles, Californie (1987–2001); Immeuble Nationale Nederlanden, Prague, République Tchèque (1992–96); Musée Guggenheim de Bilbao, Bilbao, Espagne (1991–97).

Steven Holl
435 Hudson Street, 4th floor
New York, New York 10014

Tel: + 1 212 989 0918
Fax: + 1 212 463 9718

Richard Meier & Partners
475 Tenth Avenue
New York, New York 10018

Tel: + 1 212 967 6060
Fax: + 1 212 967 3207

François de Menil
21 East 40th Street
New York, New York 10017

Tel: + 1 212 779 3400
Fax: + 1 212 779 3414

Steven Holl

Born in 1947 in Bremerton, Washington. B. Arch., University of Washington, 1970, in Rome and at the Architectural Association in London (1976). Began his career in California and opened his own office in New York in 1976. Has taught at the University of Washington, Syracuse University and, since 1981, at Columbia University. Notable buildings: Hybrid Building, Seaside, Florida (1984–88); Berlin AGB Library, Berlin, Germany, competition entry (1988); Void Space/Hinged Space, Housing, Nexus World, Fukuoka, Japan (1989–91); Stretto House, Dallas, Texas (1989–92); Makuhari Housing, Chiba, Japan (1992–97); Chapel of St. Ignatius, Seattle University, Seattle, Washington (1994–97); Museum of Contemporary Art, Helsinki, Finland (1993–1998). Current work also includes the Cranbrook Institute of Science, Bloomfield Hills, Michigan (1998).

Steven Holl wurde 1947 in Bremerton, Washington, geboren, studierte Architektur an der University of Washington (B. Arch. 1970), dann in Rom. 1976 schloß er sein Studium an der Architectural Association in London ab, war zunächst in Kalifornien tätig und machte sich 1976 mit einem eigenen Büro in New York selbständig. Lehraufträge an der University of Washington, der Syracuse University und (seit 1981) an der Columbia University. Wichtige Bauten: Hybrid Building, Seaside, Florida (1984–88); Amerika-Gedenkbibliothek Berlin, Wettbewerbsprojekt (1988); Void Space/Hinged Space, Mietwohnhäuser, Nexus World, Fukuoka, Japan (1989–91); Stretto House, Dallas, Texas (1989–92); Makuhari Mietwohnhäuser, Chiba, Japan (1992–97); Chapel of St. Ignatius, Seattle University, Seattle, Washington (1994–97); Museum für Gegenwartskunst, Helsinki, Finnland (1993–98). Zu den neuesten Projekten gehört das Cranbrook Institute of Science, Bloomfield Hills, Michigan (1998).

Né en 1947 à Bremerton, Washington. Étudie à l'Université de Washington (B.A. en 1970), à Rome et à l'Architectural Association à Londres (1976). Débute en Californie et ouvre sa propre agence à New York en 1976. Enseigne à l'Université de Washington, Syracuse University, et depuis 1981 à Columbia University. Principales réalisations: Hybrid Building, Seaside, Floride (1984–88); Bibliothèque AGB, Berlin, Allemagne, projet de concours (1988); Void Space/Hinged Space, logements, Nexus World, Fukuoka, Japon (1989–91); Stretto House, Dallas, Texas (1989–92); immeuble de logements Makuhari, Chiba, Japon (1992–97); chapelle Saint-Ignace, Université de Seattle, Seattle, Washington (1994–97); musée d'art contemporain d'Helsinki, Finlande (1993–98). Travaille actuellement sur le Cranbrook Institute of Science, Bloomfield Hills, Michigan (1998).

Richard Meier

Born in Newark, New Jersey in 1934, Richard Meier received his architectural training at Cornell University, and worked in the office of Marcel Breuer (1961–63) before establishing his own practice in 1963. Pritzker Prize, 1984; Royal Gold Medal, 1988. Notable buildings: The Atheneum, New Harmony, Indiana (1975–79); Museum for the Decorative Arts, Frankfurt am Main, Germany (1979–85); High Museum of Art, Atlanta, Georgia (1980–83); Canal+ Headquarters, Paris, France (1988–92); City Hall and Library, The Hague, The Netherlands (1986–95); Barcelona Museum of Contemporary Art, Barcelona, Spain (1987–95); Getty Center, Los Angeles, California (1984–97). Current work includes a U.S. Courthouse and Federal Building, Phoenix, Arizona (1995–2000).

Richard Meier wurde 1934 in Newark, New Jersey geboren, studierte Architektur an der Cornell University und arbeitete 1961–63 im Büro von Marcel Breuer, bevor er sich 1963 selbständig machte. Auszeichnungen: Pritzker Prize 1984, Royal Gold Medal 1988. Wichtige Bauten: Atheneum, New Harmony, Indiana (1975–79); Museum für Kunsthandwerk, Frankfurt/Main (1979–85); High Museum of Art, Atlanta, Georgia (1980–83); Hauptsitz von Canal+, Paris, Frankreich (1988–92); Rathaus und Bibliothek, Den Haag, Niederlande (1986–95); Museum für Zeitgenössische Kunst, Barcelona, Spanien (1987–95); Getty Center, Los Angeles, Kalifornien (1984–97). Neueste Bauten sind u.a. das US Courthouse und Bundesbauten in Phoenix, Arizona (1995–2000).

Né à Newark, New Jersey, en 1934, Richard Meier a étudié l'architecture à Cornell University, et travaillé dans l'agence de Marcel Breuer (1961–63) avant de s'installer à son compte en 1963. Pritzker Prize, 1984. Royal Gold Medal, 1988. Principales réalisations: The Atheneum, New Harmony, Indiana (1975–79); Musée des Arts décoratifs, Francfort sur le Main, Allemagne (1979–85); High Museum of Art, Atlanta, Georgie (1980–83); siège social de Canal+, Paris, France (1988–92); mairie et bibliothèque à La Hague, Pays-Bas (1986–95); musée d'art contemporain de Barcelone, Espagne (1987–95); Getty Center, Los Angeles, Californie (1984–97). Actuellement en cours de construction: palais de justice et immeubles fédéraux, Phoenix, Arizona (1995–2000).

François de Menil

Born in 1945, François de Menil grew up in Houston, Texas. He briefly attended Columbia University in New York in 1965 before making films about the sculptors Jean Tinguely, Niki de Saint Phalle and Mark di Suvero. He subsequently created a firm called FDM Productions, which produced four Broadway plays. In 1987, he obtained a Bachelor of Architecture degree from The Cooper Union, and worked in the offices of Richard Meier and Kohn Pederson Fox before founding his own firm in New York in 1991. Aside from the Byzantine Fresco Chapel Museum published here, he has completed retail shops for Bottega Veneta in Kyoto, Tokyo, Fukuoka, Kobe, Yokohama, New Jersey, and New York. He renovated the offices of Esquire Magazine in New York (1993) and Wells/BDDP also in New York (1997).

François de Menil wurde 1945 geboren und wuchs in Houston, Texas, auf. Er besuchte nur kurz die Columbia University, New York (1965), bevor er sich dem Dokumentarfilm zuwandte. Er realisierte Filme über die Bildhauer Jean Tinguely, Niki de Saint Phalle und Mark di Suvero und gründete dann die FDM-Produktionsgesellschaft, die vier Broadway-Stücke produzierte. Schließlich studierte er Architektur an der Cooper Union (B. Arch. 1987) und arbeitete bei Richard Meier und Kohn Pederson Fox, bevor er 1991 sein eigenes Büro in New York gründete. De Menil hat außer dem hier vorgestellten Kapellen-Museum zahlreiche Boutiquen ausgestattet, u.a. für Bottega Veneta in Kyoto, Tokio, Fukuoka, Kobe, Yokohama, New Jersey und New York. Er modernisierte die Büros des Esquire Magazine in New York (1993) und von Wells/BDDP, ebenfalls in New York (1997).

Né en 1945, François de Menil a été élevé à Houston, Texas. Il étudie brièvement à Columbia University, New York, en 1965, avant de réaliser des films sur les sculpteurs Jean Tinguely, Niki de Saint Phalle et Mark di Suvero. Il crée par la suite une société, FDM Productions, qui produit quatre spectacles à Broadway. En 1987, il obtient son B.A. en architecture à Cooper Union, et travaille dans les agences de Richard Meier et de Kohn Pederson Fox, avant de créer sa propre agence à New York en 1991. En dehors de la chapelle-musée des fresques byzantines publié ici, il a réalisé des boutiques pour Bottega Veneta à Kyoto, Tokyo, Fukuoka, Kobe, Yokohama, New Jersey et New York. Il a rénové les bureaux d'Esquire Magazine (1993) et de l'agence de publicité Wells/BDDP (1997), également à New York.

Auburn Rural Studio
PO Box 476
Greensboro, Alabama 36744

Tel: +1 334 624 4483
Fax: + 1 334 624 6015

Mockbee/Coker Architects
360 East North Street
Canton, Mississippi

Tel: + 1 601 859 7538

Morphosis
2041 Colorado Avenue
Santa Monica, California 90404

Tel: + 1 310 453 2247
Fax: + 1 310 829 3270

Eric Owen Moss Architects
8557 Higuera Street
Culver City, California 90232

Tel: + 1 310 839 1199
Fax: + 1 310 839 7922

Sambo Mockbee and the Rural Studio

Sambo Mockbee, born in 1945, founded Mockbee/
Coker Architects, based in Canton, Mississippi and in
Memphis, Tennessee with Coleman Coker in 1978. The
firm has completed a number of structures, including
the Barton House and the Cook House, both located
in Mississippi. They have a considerable reputation
in the region, established through their contemporary
interpretations of local architecture. Sambo Mockbee
has taught at Yale and at the University of Oklahoma,
and has been a Professor of Architecture at Auburn
University since 1991. He created the Rural Studio in
1993 "to extend the study of architecture into a socially
responsible context" for twelve of his students each
quarter. He seems to have passed on to the Rural
Studio the vocabulary of simple materials and regional
inspiration for which Mockbee/Coker is known.

Sambo Mockbee, 1945 geboren, gründete 1978 zusammen mit Coleman Coker das Büro Mockbee/Coker
Architects in Canton, Mississippi, mit einem Zweitbüro
in Memphis, Tennessee. Das Büro hat u.a. die Häuser
Barton und Cook in Mississippi gebaut und sich in
der Region mit der Neuinterpretation örtlicher Bautradi-
tionen einen Namen gemacht. Sambo Mockbee hat
in Yale und an der University of Oklahoma gelehrt und
ist seit 1991 Professor für Architektur an der Auburn
University. 1993 gründete er das Büro Rural Studio,
»um das Architekturstudium in einen sozialverantwort-
lichen Kontext zu stellen« – und zwar in jedem Quartal
für zwölf Studenten. Offenbar hat er die Formensprache
der einfachen Materialien und der regionalen Inspiration, für die Mockbee/Coker bekannt sind, auch mit ins
Rural Studio genommen.

Né en 1945, Sambo Mockbee a fondé avec Coleman
Coker, en 1978, l'agence Mockbee/Coker Architects,
basée à Canton, Mississippi, et à Memphis, Tennesse.
Ils ont réalisé un certains nombres de projets, dont la
Barton House et la Cook House, toutes deux dans le
Mississippi. Ils sont très connus dans la région pour
leur interprétation contemporaine de l'architecture
locale. Sambo Mockbee a enseigné à Yale, à l'Université
de l'Oklahoma, et professe l'architecture, à l'Université
d'Auburn depuis 1991. Il crée le Rural Studio en 1993
«pour étendre l'étude de l'architecture dans un contexte
socialement responsable», pour douze de ses étudiants
chaque trimestre. Il semble avoir transmis au Rural
Studio le vocabulaire à base de matériaux simples et
d'inspiration régionale pour lequel Mockbee/Coker
s'est fait connaître.

Morphosis

Morphosis principal Thom Mayne, born in Connecticut
in 1944, received his B. Arch. in 1968 (USC), and
his M. Arch. degree at Harvard in 1978. He founded
Morphosis in 1971, and formalized his partnership with
Michael Rotondi in 1980. They parted in 1991, and
Rotondi created his own firm, RoTo. Thom Mayne has
taught at UCLA, Harvard, and Yale and SCI-Arc, of
which he was a founding Board Member. Based in
Santa Monica, California, some of the main buildings
of Morphosis are the Kate Mantilini Restaurant, Beverly
Hills, California (1986); Cedar's Sinai Comprehensive
Cancer Care Center, Beverly Hills, California (1987);
Crawford Residence, Montecito, California (1987–92);
Golf Club in Chiba Prefecture, Japan (1988–92);
Yuzen Vintage Car Museum, West Hollywood, California
(project, 1992); as well as the more recent Blades
Residence, Santa Barbara, California (1992–96),
the Sun Tower, Seoul, Korea (1995–97), and Hypo Alpe
Adria Center, Klagenfurt, Austria (1995–98).

Thom Mayne, Direktor von Morphosis in Santa Monica,
Kalifornien, wurde 1944 in Connecticut geboren.
Er studierte Architektur an der University of Southern
California (B. Arch. 1968) und in Harvard (M. Arch.
1978). Thom Mayne gründete 1971 Morphosis, 1980
machte er seine Partnerschaft mit Michael Rotondi
offiziel; 1991 trennten sich die beiden und Rotondi
gründete sein eigenes Büro RoTo. Mayne hat an der
University of California, Los Angeles (UCLA), in Harvard
und Yale gelehrt sowie am Southern California Institute
of Architecture (SCI-Arc), das er mitbegründet hat. Zu
den Hauptwerken von Morphosis zählen: Kate Mantilini
Restaurant, Beverly Hills, Kalifornien (1986); Cedar's
Sinai Comprehensive Cancer Care Center, Beverly
Hills (1987); Crawford House, Montecito, Kalifornien
(1987–92); Golf Club, Chiba Prefecture, Japan (1988–92);
Yuzen Vintage Car Museum, West Hollywood,
Kalifornien (Projekt, 1992) und in jüngerer Zeit die
Blades Residence in Santa Barbara, Kalifornien
(1992–96), der Sun Tower in Seoul, Korea (1995–97)
und das Hypo Alpe Adria Center in Klagenfurt,
Österreich (1995–98).

Principal associé de Morphosis, Thom Mayne, né au
Connecticut en 1944, passe son diplôme d'architecte
en 1968 (USC) et son M.A. à Harvard en 1978. Il fonda
Morphosis en 1971, et s'associa en 1980 avec Michael
Rotondi. Ils se séparèrent en 1991, et Rotondi créa
sa propre entreprise, RoTo. Thom Mayne a enseigné à
l'UCLA, à Harvard, Yale et au SCI-Arc, dont il est l'un
des fondateurs. Morphosis est basé à Santa Monica,
Californie. Principales réalisations: Kate Mantilini
Restaurant, Beverly Hills, Californie (1986); Cedar's
Sinai Comprehensive Cancer Care Center, Beverly Hills,
Californie (1987); Crawford Residence, Montecito,
Californie (1987–92); Golf Club à Chiba Prefecture,
Japon (1988–92); Yuzen Vintage Car Museum, West
Hollywood, Californie (projet, 1992), Blades Residence,
Santa Barbara, Californie (1992–96), Sun Tower, Séoul,
Corée-du-Sud (1995–97) et Hypo Alpe Adria Center,
Klagenfurt, Autriche (1995–98).

Eric Owen Moss

Born in Los Angeles, California in 1943, Eric Owen Moss
received his B.A. degree from UCLA in 1965, and his
M. Arch. in 1968. He also received an M. Arch. degree
at Harvard in 1972. He has been a Professor of Design
at the Southern California Institute of Architecture
since 1973. He opened his own firm in Los Angeles,
California, in 1973. His built work includes the Central
Housing Office, University of California at Irvine, Irvine,
California (1986–89); Lindblade Tower (1987–89);
Paramount Laundry (1987–89); Gary Group (1988–90);
The Box (1990–94); IRS Building (1993–94); and
Samitaur (1994–96) – all in Culver City, California.

Eric Owen Moss wurde 1943 in Los Angeles, Kalifornien,
geboren. Er studierte Architektur an der UCLA (B.A.
1965, M. Arch. 1968) und in Harvard (M. Arch. 1972).
Seit 1973 ist er Professor für Gestaltung am Southern
California Institute of Architecture. 1973 Gründung des
eigenen Büros in Los Angeles, Kalifornien. Zu seinen
Bauten gehören: Central Housing Office der University
of California in Irvine, Kalifornien (1986–89); Lindblade
Tower(1987–89); Paramount Laundry (1987–89);
Gary Group (1988–90); The Box (1990–94); IRS Building
(1993–94) und Samitaur (1994–96) – alle in Culver City,
Kalifornien.

Né à Los Angeles, Californie, en 1943, Eric Owen Moss
est diplômé d'architecture de l'UCLA (1965), et a passé
deux Masters en architecture, en 1968 à l'UCLA et en
1972 à Harvard. Il enseigne le dessin au Southern
California Institute of Architecture depuis 1973, et a
ouvert son propre cabinet à Los Angeles, Californie, la
même année. Principales réalisations: Central Housing
Office, University of California à Irvine, Californie
(1986–89); Lindblade Tower (1987–89); Paramount
Laundry (1987–89); Gary Group (1988–90); The
Box (1990–94); IRS Building (1993–94) et Samitaur
(1994–96) – tous situés à Culver City, Californie.

I.M. Pei, Architect
600 Madison Avenue
New York, New York 10022

Tel: + 1 212 751 3122
Fax: + 1 212 872 5443

RoTo Architects
600 Moulton Ave #405
Los Angeles, CA 90031

Tel : + 1 213 226 1112
Fax : + 1 213 226 1105

Thompson and Rose Architects
1430 Massachusetts Avenue
Cambridge, Massuchusetts 02138

Tel: + 1 617 876 9966
Fax: + 1 617 876 9922

Ieoh Ming Pei

Born in 1917 in Canton (now Guangzhou), China. Pei came to the United States in 1935. B. Arch., M.I.T. (1940); M. Arch., Harvard (1942); Doctorate, Harvard (1946). Formed I.M. Pei & Associates, 1955. AIA Gold Medal, 1979; Pritzker Prize, 1983; Praemium Imperiale, Japan, 1989. Notable buildings: National Center for Atmospheric Research, Boulder, Colorado (1961–67); Federal Aviation Agency Air Traffic Control Towers, fifty buildings, various locations (1962–70); John F. Kennedy Library, Boston, Massachusetts (1965–79); National Gallery of Art, East Building, Washington, D.C. (1968–78); Bank of China Tower, Hong Kong (1982–89); Grand Louvre, Paris, France (1983–93); Rock and Roll Hall of Fame, Cleveland, Ohio (1993–95); Miho Museum, Shigaraki, Shiga, Japan (1992–97). Current projects include a museum of modern art in Luxembourg.

1917 in Kanton (heute Guangzhou) in China geboren, kam Pei 1935 in die USA. Er studierte am M.I.T. (B. Arch. 1940) und in Harvard (M. Arch. 1942), wo er 1946 mit einem Doktorat abschloß. Gründete 1955 I.M. Pei & Associates. 1979 erhielt er die AIA Gold Medal, 1983 den Pritzker Prize, 1989 den Praemium Imperiale, Japan. Wichtige Bauten: National Center for Atmospheric Research, Boulder, Colorado (1961–67); Federal Aviation Agency, 50 Luftkontrolltürme an verschiedenen Flughäfen (1962–70); John F. Kennedy Library, Boston, Massa-chusetts (1965–79); National Gallery of Art, East Building, Washington, D.C. (1968–78); Bank of China Tower, Hongkong (1982–89); Umbau und Pyramide des Louvre, Paris (1983–93); Rock and Roll Hall of Fame, Cleveland, Ohio (1993–95); Miho Museum, Shigaraki, Shiga, Japan (1992–97). Zu seinen neuesten Projekten zählt das Museum für moderne Kunst in Luxemburg.

Né en 1917 à Canton, aujourd'hui Guangzhou (Chine), Pei arrive aux États-Unis en 1935. Diplôme d'architecture au M.I.T. (1940), Master à Harvard (1942), Doctorat à Harvard (1946). Crée I.M. Pei & Associates en 1955. Médaille d'or AIA, 1979; Pritzker Prize, 1983; Prix Impérial du Japon, 1989. Principales réalisations: National Center for Atmospheric Research, Boulder, Colorado (1961–67); Federal Aviation Agency Air Traffic Control Towers: 50 tours de contrôle à travers les États-Unis (1962–70); Bibliothèque John F. Kennedy, Boston, Massachusetts (1965–79); National Gallery of Art, East Building, Washington D. C. (1968–78); Tour de la Banque de Chine, Hongkong (1982–89); Grand Louvre, Paris, France (1983–93); Rock and Roll Hall of Fame, Cleveland, Ohio (1993–95); Musée Miho, Shigaraki, Shiga, Japon (1992–97). Il travaille actuellement sur un projet de musée d'art moderne au Luxembourg.

RoTo

Born in 1949 in Los Angeles, Michael Rotondi received his B. Arch. from the Southern California Institute of Architecture (SCI-Arc) in 1973. He worked with DMJM in Los Angeles (1973–76), and collaborated with Peter de Bretteville and Craig Hodgetts from 1974 to 1976. He was Director of the Graduate Design Faculty at SCI-Arc from 1976 to 1987. A principal of Morphosis with Thom Mayne, Michael Rotondi has been the Director of SCI-Arc since 1987. He created his present firm, RoTo, with Clark Stevens in 1991. Stevens received his M. Arch. degree from Harvard in 1989 and worked at Morphosis beginning in 1987. Projects include CDLT 1,2, Cedar Lodge Terrace, Silverlake, California (1991); the Nicola Restaurant, Los Angeles, California (1992–93); the Teiger House, Somerset County, New Jersey (1990–95); and the Warehouse C and Public Gardens, Nagasaki, Japan (1994–97)

Michael Rotondi wurde 1949 in Los Angeles geboren und studierte Architektur am Southern California Institute of Architecture (SCI-Arc), das er 1973 mit dem B. Arch. abschloß. Zwischen 1973 und 1976 war er für DMJM in Los Angeles tätig und arbeitete von 1974 bis 1976 in Gemeinschaft mit Peter de Bretteville und Craig Hodgetts. Von 1976 bis 1987 leitete er die Graduate Design Faculty an der SCI-Arc, deren Rektor er seit 1987 ist. Partner von Thom Mayne im Büro Morphosis von 1980 bis 1991. 1991 gründete er zusammen mit Clark Stevens RoTo Architects. Clark Stevens – der seit 1987 bei Morphosis arbeitete – schloß 1989 sein Harvard Studium mit dem M. Arch. ab. Projekte: CDLT 1,2, Cedar Lodge Terrace, Silverlake, Kalifornien (1991), das Nicola Restaurant, Los Angeles, Kalifornien (1992–93), das Teiger House, Somerset County, New Jersey (1990–95) und das Warehouse C and Public Gardens, Nagasaki, Japan (1994–97).

Né en 1949 à Los Angeles, Michael Rotondi est diplômé en architecture du Southern California Institute of Architecture (SCI-Arc) en 1973. Il travaille à Los Angeles pour DMJM (1973–76), et collabore avec Peter de Bretteville et Craig Hodgetts de 1974 à 1976. Directeur de la faculté de design du SCI-Arc, de 1976 à 1987. Principal fondateur de Morphosis avec Thom Mayne, il dirige le SCI-Arc depuis 1987. 1991 il crée son agence actuelle, RoTo, avec Clark Stevens. Stevens recut son M.A. en architecture à Harvard en 1989, et travaille depuis 1987 pour Morphosis. Parmi ses projets: CLDT 1,2, Cedar Lodge Terrace, Silverlake, Californie (1991); Nicola Restaurant (Los Angeles, California, 1992–93); Teiger House, Somerset County, New Jersey (1990–95); Warehouse C and Public Gardens, Nagasaki, Japan (1994–97).

Thompson and Rose

Born in 1960, Maryann Thompson received her B.A. degree in Architecture at Princeton, and Masters degrees in Landscape Architecture and Architecture from Harvard. Her husband and partner, Charles Rose, born in 1960, also attended Princeton, and obtained his Master of Architecture from Harvard. Their com-pleted work includes the Hartsbrook School, Hadley, Massachusetts (1987–89); Woodland Dormitories, Kenyon College, Gambier, Ohio (1993); Gemini Consulting Offices, Cambridge, Massachusetts (1996); Atlantic Center for the Arts, New Smyrna Beach, Florida, (1994–97); Straitsview Farm, San Juan Island, Washington (1997); the Bartholomew County Veteran's Memorial, Columbus, Indiana (1997) and the Residence at 518 West 22nd Street, New York, New York (1997–98).

Maryann Thompson (geb. 1960) studierte Architektur in Princeton (B. A.) und Landschaftsarchitektur sowie Architektur in Harvard (M. Arch.). Ihr Ehemann und Büropartner Charles Rose (geb. 1960) studierte eben-falls in Princeton und schloß sein Studium in Harvard mit einem M. Arch. ab. Zu ihren realisierten Bauten gehören: Hartsbrook School in Hadley, Massuchusetts (1987–89); Woodland Dormitories, Kenyon College, Gambier, Ohio (1993); Bürohaus Gemini Consulting, Cambridge, Massachusetts (1996); Atlantic Center for the Arts, New Smyrna Beach, Florida (1994–97); Straitsview Farm, San Juan Island, Washington (1997); das Bartholomew County Veteran's Memorial, Columbus, Indiana (1997) und ein Galerie/Wohnhaus-projekt in New York, Residence at 518 West 22nd Street, New York (1997–98).

Née en 1960, Maryann Thompson a passé son B. A. en architecture à Princeton, et ses M.A. en architecture du paysage et architecture à Harvard. Son mari et associé, Charles Rose, né en 1960, a suivi la même filière. Parmi leurs réalisations: Hartsbrook School, Hadley, Massachusetts (1987–89); Woodland Dormitories, Kenyon College, Gambier, Ohio (1993); Gemini Consulting Offices, Cambridge, Massachusetts (1996); Atlantic Center for the Arts, New Smyrna Beach, Floride (1994–97); Straitsview Farm, San Juan Island, Washington (1997); le Bartholomew County, Veteran's Memorial; Columbus, Indiana (1997) et une residence à New York, 518 West 22nd Street, New York (1997–98).

Bibliography | Bibliographie

Cook, Peter and George Rand: *Morphosis, Buildings and Projects.* Rizzoli, New York, 1989.

Dixon, John Morris: "The Santa Monica School. What's Its Lasting Contribution?," *Progressive Architecture,* May 1995.

Frampton, Kenneth, Charles Jencks and Richard Meier: *Richard Meier, Buildings and Projects, 1979–1989.* St. Martin's Press, New York, 1990.

Futagawa, Yukio (editor): "Frank O. Gehry," *GA Architect n°10,* A.D.A. Edita, Tokyo, 1993.

Futagawa, Yukio (editor): "Steven Holl," *GA Architect n°11,* A.D.A. Edita, Tokyo, 1993.

Giovanni, Joseph: "Is Richard Meier Really Modern?," *Architecture,* February 1996.

Giovanni, Joseph: "Modern Reliquary," *Architecture,* April 1997.

Goldberger, Paul: "Michael Rotondi, A Contemporary Villa Embraces the New Jersey Landscape," *Architectural Digest,* March 1997.

Steven Holl. GA Document Extra 06, ADA Edita, Tokyo, 1996.

Holl, Steven: *Intertwining.* Princeton Architectural Press, New York, 1996.

Huxtable, Ada Louise: *The Unreal America, Architecture and Illusion.* The New Press, New York, 1997.

Jencks, Charles: *Heteropolis, Los Angeles, the Riots and the Strange Beauty of Hetero-Architecture.* Academy Editions, London, 1993.

Jencks, Charles (editor): *Frank O. Gehry, Individual Imagination and Cultural Conservatism.* Academy Editions, London, 1995.

Jencks, Charles: "Gehry in Bilbao," *Interiors,* August 1997.

Jerde, Jon (preface): *Steven Ehrlich, Contemporary World Architects.* Rockport Publishers, Rockport, Massachusetts, 1995.

LeBlanc, Sydney: "From Humble Sources, Earthy Elegance Springs," *The New York Times,* April 18, 1996.

Los Angeles, World Cities. Academy Editions, London, 1994.

Meier, Richard (forward by Joseph Rykwert): *Richard Meier Architect, 1964/1984.* Rizzoli, New York, 1984.

Moonan, Wendy: "A Mathematical Ordering System Helped Roto Architects Sculpt a Complex Scheme," *Architectural Record,* April 1997.

Moss, Eric Owen: *Buildings and Projects, 1991.* Rizzoli, New York.

Eric Owen Moss. Architectural Monographs N° 20. Academy Editions, London, 1993.

Moss, Eric Owen: "1974–1994," *Architecture and Urbanism (A+U),* 94:11.

Steele, James: *Los Angeles Architecture, The Contemporary Condition.* Phaidon Press, London, 1993.

Steele, James: *Eric Owen Moss.* Architectural Monographs, n° 29, Academy Editions, Ernst & Sohn, London, 1993.

Weinstein, Richard: *Morphosis, Buildings and Projects, 1989–1992.* Rizzoli, New York, 1994.

Zaera, Alejandro: "Frank O. Gehry," *El Croquis, 74/75,* Madrid, 1995.

Index

Credits | Fotonachweis | Crédits photographiques

l. = left | links | à gauche
r. = right | rechts | à droite
t. = top | oben | en haut
c. = center | Mitte | centre
b. = bottom | unten | en bas